THE BOOK OF
SILVERTON

THE BOOK OF
SILVERTON

PORTRAIT OF AN EXE
VALLEY PARISH

SILVERTON LOCAL HISTORY SOCIETY

HALSGROVE

First published in Great Britain in 2000

Copyright © 2000 Silverton Local History Society

British Library Cataloguing-in-Publication Data
A CIP record for this title is available from the British Library

ISBN 1 84114 066 X

HALSGROVE
PUBLISHING, MEDIA AND DISTRIBUTION

Halsgrove House
Lower Moor Way
Tiverton, Devon EX16 6SS
Tel: 01884 243242
Fax: 01884 243325
email: sales@halsgrove.com
website: http://www.halsgrove.com

Printed and bound in Great Britain by Bookcraft Ltd, Midsomer Norton.

FOREWORD

Silverton is a parish whose population continues to expand (as does that of the village itself): and its character is changing constantly. Even in a time-span so historically short as 30 years, the Paper Mill which was once a major source of employment has finally succumbed to altered economic realities; its village smithy is now closed and reassembled in Tiverton Museum (and, with the death of its last blacksmith, the gift of wart-charming possibly departed forever?). The advent of the car, which generated two garages and a set of petrol pumps to meet its needs in the village, has been inadequate to retain those businesses profitably within Silverton (but has endowed the village with a dormitory function for Exeter and Tiverton).

Yet the identity of Silverton persists organically, because the flow of its history remains creative and vigorous. For that flow to be animated, however, requires periodic assessment and recording of it by thoughtful, industrious and caring Silvertonians at some focal moment, for the lasting benefit both of their own contemporaries and of those who come after them.

How grateful we should be, therefore, to them for their labours, skill, sensitivity and affection for Silverton, made manifest in this timely book.

SIR ROBIN MAXWELL-HYSLOP
SILVERTON, 2000

Silverton Church, drawn from nature and on stone by W. Spreat junr in 1842 from Picturesque Sketches of Churches of Devon. *This gentleman had a studio at 263 High Street, Exeter. Note that this was drawn before the church was rebuilt in 1862/3.*

A view of lower High Street, showing Charity Cottages adorned with a creeper on the right, and French's shop on the left. Among the children are Elaine Gooding (née Stephens) and her brother Fred. Standing in the doorway on the right are Minnie Nicholls (née Ford) and Sylvia Carpenter (née Crabtree).

A view of The Square in the 1920s showing some of the thatched cottages. Note the baker's cart in the centre.

CONTENTS

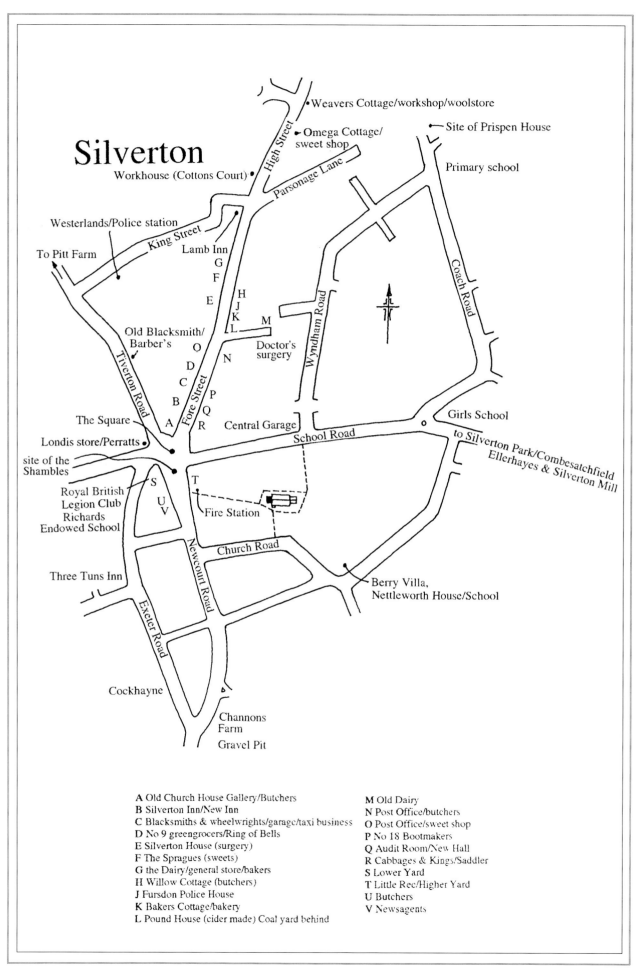

Silverton

Weavers Cottage/workshop/woolstore

Site of Prispen House

Omega Cottage/ sweet shop

Primary school

Workhouse (Cottons Court)

High Street

Parsonage Lane

Westerlands/Police station

King Street

Coach Road

To Pitt Farm

Lamb Inn

G
F
E

H
J
K
L
M

Old Blacksmith/ Barber's

O
D
C
B
A

N
P
Q
R

Doctor's surgery

Wyndham Road

Tiverton Road

Fore Street

The Square

Central Garage

Girls School

Londis store/Perratts

School Road

to Silverton Park/Combesatchfield Ellerhayes & Silverton Mill

site of the Shambles

S
U
V

T

Royal British Legion Club Richards Endowed School

Fire Station

Newcourt Road

Church Road

Three Tuns Inn

Berry Villa, Nettleworth House/School

Exeter Road

Cockhayne

Channons Farm

Gravel Pit

A Old Church House Gallery/Butchers
B Silverton Inn/New Inn
C Blacksmiths & wheelwrights/garage/taxi business
D No 9 greengrocers/Ring of Bells
E Silverton House (surgery)
F The Spragues (sweets)
G the Dairy/general store/bakers
H Willow Cottage (butchers)
J Fursdon Police House
K Bakers Cottage/bakery
L Pound House (cider made) Coal yard behind

M Old Dairy
N Post Office/butchers
O Post Office/sweet shop
P No 18 Bootmakers
Q Audit Room/New Hall
R Cabbages & Kings/Saddler
S Lower Yard
T Little Rec/Higher Yard
U Butchers
V Newsagents

ACKNOWLEDGEMENTS

During the past three years the Silverton Local History Society has made various appeals, and displayed photographs and slides at village meetings in order to obtain information for this book. A great many offers of help have been received in the form of information, items of local interest and photographs. Some of these items have been of great sentimental value, and although by no means everything could possibly be included in this volume, where possible it has been recorded so that it may be used by future researchers interested in the history of Silverton and families of the parish.

Thanks must go to the following for passing on information and loaning photographs for scanning and storing: John Abrahams, Geoff Allen, Bill and Audrey Atkinson, Joan, Francis, James and Thomas Ayshford, Bill and Audrey Barker (USA), Dr Avis Blundell-Jones, Richard Bond, Helen Boucher, Eileen Brook, Ron Bryant, Gwen Carroll, Gordon and Mary Chudley, Peter Crabtree, Ann Crew, Bill Croome, Edward Davies, Nora Davies, Fred Down, Edith Diamond, Phyllis Dymond, Joyce Eldridge, Dr Charlotte Foster, Joan Frankpitt, Peggy French, Steve French, Rod and Chris Furlong, Eric Gill, Pearl Gill, Brian Gooding, Eva Gooding, Peter and Ann Gundry, Bernard and Gwen Hawkins, Jack Haydon, Brian Hooper, June Hutchings, Monica Hyde, Ruby Isaac, Lil Jefferson, John Leach, Dr Richard Leete, Tim Lewer, Col J. Massey, Simon and Linda Molineux, Sir Robin Maxwell-Hyslop, Martin Nash, Alison Newton, Naomi Nicholson, Graham and Ruth Pauley (New Zealand), David Petherick, Dave Piney, Walter Pye, Roy Rice, Alec Rolls, Betty Scagell, Grace Selley, Colin Selley, Robert Seward, Marjorie Shere, Susan Shere, Donald Short, Clifford Skinner, Lawrence Skinner, Percy and Elaine Stevens, Bertha Stradling, Frank and Margaret Sutton, Bill and Joan Traill, Sylvia Tree, George Tully, Mary Vile, Archie Ware, Betty West, Tim West, John and Ros White, Arthur Williams, Edward Woolway, George Woolway, and the late Eileen Stradling.

Election day, 1923. The Conservative office was in Archie Tremlett's cottage and the Liberal office in the Old Church House.

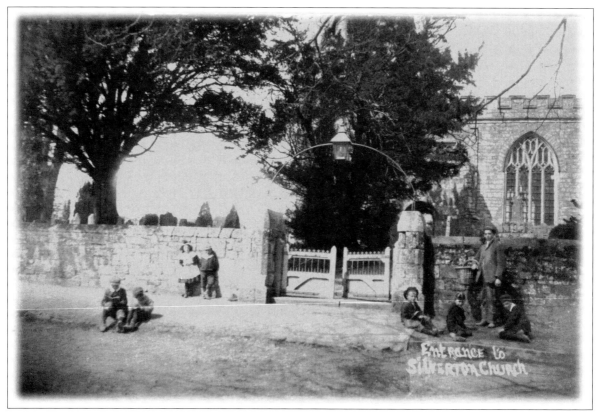

Village children playing outside the church in the late 1800s.

Harvest time on Symonds Farm, c.1920.

ACKNOWLEDGEMENTS

Special thanks to Mr Heath Nickels, Headmaster of Silverton Church of England Primary School and the following members of the 1999 senior class, whose 'Leavers Projects' provided information used in the compilation of this book: Alice Hannaford, Jennie Harris, Rosie Heap, Glyn Horton, Adam Langabeer, Abigail Laverick, Tom Lawson, Jemma Miller, Naomi Scott and Lara Snowdon. Mention must be made of the Silverton website on the Internet which has been produced by Miles Snowdon. Miles spent much time incorporating the flyer as soon as it was received from the printers, so that descendants of Silvertonians throughout the world could be informed of, and hopefully order, this book. Thank you Miles! A special mention to Michael Griffin, for the excellent map included in this publication, and to Ron Bowerman and Peggy Moore for their in-depth knowledge of the village, and for the supply of far more stories and memories than could ever be included in one volume!

I am extremely grateful to my fellow members of The Silverton Local History Society, without whose efforts this book would never have reached the publishers: Sheila Cameron, Jonathan Ayshford, Dick Passmore, Peter Smith, John Swain, and in particular Jack Tree. Jack's love of Silverton, knowledge of photography, and willingness to purchase specialised equipment for his computer, has enabled a wide range of photographs to be included. Also to Phyllis Swain who has kept us refreshed with coffee and shortbread during our many meetings at 'Wayside'! Sadly one very enthusiastic member of our group, Bernard Ayshford, developed cancer, and died while the book was taking shape. Thank you Bernard, your contribution and special knowledge of Silverton were valued and are greatly missed.

Although the book is now complete, the Society is most anxious that the research into the history of Silverton should continue so that we can create an archive for the benefit of the village. Please continue passing on information and photographs so that this can become a reality. Many of the photographs included in this volume contain people whose names are not known. Should you be able to put a name to a face, please pass the information on to a member of the Society so that it may be recorded.

Finally it is impossible to mention everyone who has helped with this venture, so apologies and a big thank you to those of you who have been inadvertently omitted.

Graham J.H. Parnell,
Silverton. August 2000

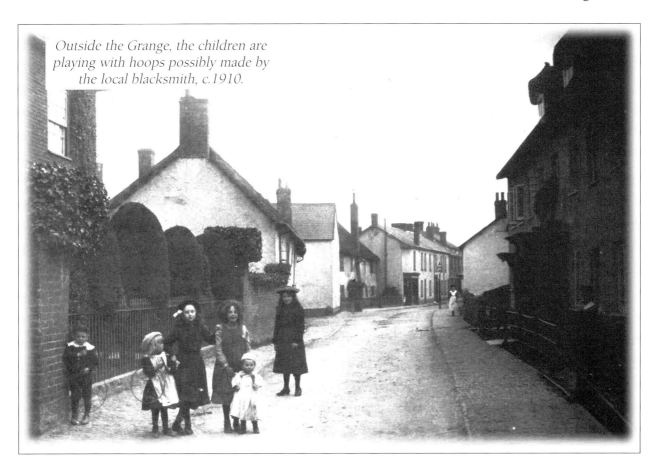

Outside the Grange, the children are playing with hoops possibly made by the local blacksmith, c.1910.

Boys playing in Fore Street in the early 1900s.

Silverton Station, c.1955. The sidings on the right of the picture were used to take raw materials (wood pulp, esparto grass, etc.) in to Silverton Mill.

Introduction
Silverton Local History Society

The Silverton Local History Society was formed by David Edmund and a number of residents on 26 October, 1981. An enthusiastic amateur historian, David was an authority on the history of the village, and had a keen interest in many other historical topics, in particular Exeter's Theatre Royal. Monthly meetings were held at Silverton Primary School, with guest speakers when David was not giving the talk himself, which he regularly illustrated with slides from his large collection.

After David's death from cancer during May 1993 when aged only 64, the Society continued under the leadership of Wilf and Joan Barnes. During 1998 a number of members decided to collate as much information as possible with the aim of publishing a book depicting village history. David's widow Jane was approached and very kindly allowed the use of the slides and photographs that David had collected over the years. It had long been his intention to write a village history, but sadly his untimely death occurred before this work commenced. This book has been written in memory of David's great love of the parish of Silverton.

The late Bernard Ayshford in 'Bonzo', his father's Austin 7 that was used to deliver newspapers.
Prior to his death Bernard was involved in the compilation of this book.

Pallbearers chatting after a funeral on The Berry, 1907. The photograph shows the number of trees that once stood on the spot but which have now disappeared.

A view of The Berry with local children in the early-20th century.

Chapter 1
Early Beginnings

How long the Silverton area has been inhabited is open to speculation. One theory takes us back to prehistoric times when ancient Britons are said to have lived at Pig's Park. This is the area to be found by walking up the lane beside the second bungalow on the north entrance to Silverdale.

Follow the footpath up the steep hill to where a hedge travels in an east/west direction making the horizontal bar of a letter T, hence the local name 'T shaped field'. Cross the stile and where the next field forms a spur into the Exe Valley is the site of earthworks, said to be the remains of the round huts. A perimeter wall would have surrounded the area, necessary to protect the livestock from wolves that lived in the woods covering the locality at this time.

It is also thought that the ancient village was situated between the area we now know as 'The Berry', and the lower land behind Channons Farm. Whichever may be regarded as the origins of Silverton it was certainly inhabited before the Romans arrived in Exeter and drove out the wild savages from the surrounding lands! No one knows whether any Romans actually settled closer to here than Exeter itself, but food grown in this area would probably have been supplied to them at their Exeter fortress and camp at Tiverton.

Many years after the Romans had departed these shores Saxons would have made their homes in clearings in the woods, and used the rich soils of the Exe Valley to grow food. They gave Silverton its name, and built a chapel shown on the 19th-century map of the village sited to the east of the chancel of the present church.

The Saxons gave the fords where the river could be crossed individual names. For example: Dulverton (Deal Ford Town), Tiverton (Two Ford Town – a ford through the Lowman and the Exe), Thorverton (Through Ford Town). The Exe west of Silverton had no natural ford by which the Saxons could cross the river from their settlement or tun. With the use of a plough, the Saxon name for which was 'sil', to reduce the height of the riverbank, a ford would have been constructed. Therefore Silverton is Plough Ford Town.

However, like the theory of the ancient settlement, this also is open to conjecture. In the Domesday Book Silverton was listed as 'Sulfreton', which is possibly 'Great Road Town'. 'Seolfre' in Saxon is silver, so it could have been 'the rich town'. Speculation over this word throughout the country is great, as Silver appears in many placenames. The *Dictionary of Modern Place Names* states that its meaning is 'farmhouse by the gully ford'. One will never know for sure, so accept the theory that appeals to you the most!

One other Saxon name is present today in Silverton, 'The Berry'. This was the name given to the area south of the church where the women, children and animals of the settlement were safe from attack.

An unusually shaped stone about twelve inches long, and eight inches in circumference at the centre, pointed at one end and flat at the other, was found by a man named Dan Godfrey, while digging a trench at Stockwell. He used it to prop open the door of his cottage in Parsonage Lane, and thought it to be a thunderbolt, as a tree close to where he had found it had recently been struck by lightening. When the local rector, the Revd J. Heald Ward, saw it he realised that man must have shaped it, and considered it to be an agricultural tool. He took it to Exeter Museum from where it was taken to an expert from the British Museum. Here it was identified as being of eyenite, the stone used for the most sacred inner circle at Stonehenge. Not known in this area, the stone must have been carried here by man and probably used in some religious ceremony. It is now being kept at the Royal Albert Museum at Exeter,

Stone tool found at Stockwell

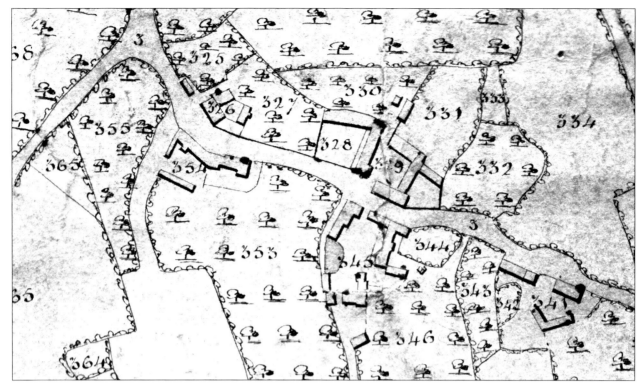

A section of the 1842 tithe map, showing the many buildings in Windmill Lane,
situated between New Barn Lane and Newcourt Road.

where it is on display in the Prehistory Gallery. However, when it was again examined in the 1960s, it was decided that it was Cornish greenstone from the area close to Camborne, and not at all related to Stonehenge.

During Saxon times the king owned the Manor of Silverton. Edward the Confessor's property was inherited by his successor, William the Conqueror, and Silverton continued in royal hands until a Plantagenet king gave it to a favourite - a Beauchamp.

John, Lord Beauchamp, died childless and Silverton was inherited by his sister Lady Cecily Turberville. During the 14th century the Beauchamp family sold to Sir John Wadham, a Justice of the Common Peace, whose only son Sir Nicholas Wadham was Governor of the Isle of Wight and attended King Henry VIII. It was possibly during this period that the cross in the churchyard would have been broken, and those at Red Cross, Stumpy Cross and Christ Cross removed, when the authority of the Pope in Rome was denied over the Church of England, and King Henry was made head of the English Church. However, generations of Silverton children have been taught that this occurred during the Civil War, when Silverton was occupied by Cromwell's army under the command of Sir Thomas Fairfax.

At this time Silverton had the status of a borough, and held a fair and a weekly market. It had far more importance in the area than the village as we know today. On his death Sir Nicholas left his estates to Sir John Strangways and Sir William Wyndham, who apportioned the rents of Silverton and Rewe seven twelfths to the Wyndhams and five twelfths to the Strangways. Various generations of the Wyndham family inherited Silverton and Sir John Wyndham (1610-68), who had nine sons and six daughters, left the estate to his eldest son, a descendant of whom was to inherit the Earldom of Egremont. When he died in 1845, he left great debts that forced the sale of the Silverton Estate. The great sale held in Exeter at the Rougemont Hotel on 27 May 1915, saw the properties finally split up and passed into various private hands.

Stone-Age tools from Devon, including in the centre the prehistoric stone tool found near Silverton.

Chapter 2
A Walk Around Silverton

Situated on a hill about eight miles north of Exeter, in the valley of the River Exe, the village of Silverton is thought to be one of the oldest in Devonshire. The main street is said to have followed the route of an early ridgeline road from Exeter to Tiverton, but was by-passed when a new road was built in the valley in the mid-19th century. This walk starts in the village Square, typically the hub of the village, where all main roads into Silverton meet.

THE SQUARE

Between the war memorial and the Royal British Legion Club the road is noticeably wide. The reason for this is that in 1894 a fire destroyed buildings that stood in the centre of the roadway, and these were never rebuilt. One of the buildings was a butcher's shop, and it is thought that boiling fat spilling over in that shop started the fire. This area was formerly known as 'The Shambles' - a name that means a district where animals are brought for slaughter, or indeed simply any place for slaughter or execution. It is possible that the practice of the butchers throwing waste from the carcasses into the street, to be eaten by dogs and pigs, also caused the area to be considered 'a shambles' in the untidy sense of the word.

Between The Shambles and Fore Street was the site of a weekly Saturday market, discontinued in

Aerial view of the centre of Silverton taken in 1967.

A 1905 photograph of The Square from Fore Street. The width of the road is well illustrated. Note the location of the Post Office in the left foreground.

The Square showing the Boys' School and Perratt's shop in the background. Mrs Fallon, the headmaster's wife, is standing in the doorway of the schoolhouse. The old school bell can clearly be seen on the roof.

Gentleman on a horse outside Bridgeman's shop in late-19th century.

Churchward's, later Strading's, bakery.
It is interesting to note a baby in a pram being pushed by a nanny in uniform.

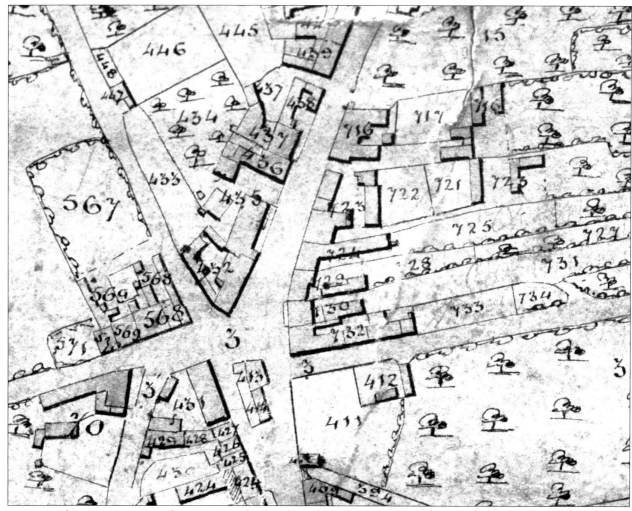

Silverton Square and vicinity, as depicted on the tithe map, showing the buildings known as 'The Shambles'. (J. Tree)

1785, and also two annual cattle fairs that took place until the late-19th century. The Shambles is shown on the parish tithe map of 1842, together with all the buildings and properties within the parish of Silverton. The 1836 Tithe Commutation Act appointed commissioners who divided the country into some 12 000 tithe districts. A large-scale map was drawn of each district and three copies of this were made. One was kept in the parish in question, and that for Silverton was still in the village until the 1950s when it was transferred to the Devon Record Office for safe keeping.

The building now occupied by the Royal British Legion, at the corner of The Square and Exeter Road, was once the Richards' Endowed School for boys. Built in 1742 from a legacy of £1200 given by John Richards, a wool merchant from the city of London, it was intended to provide education for the poor children of the parish. Above the window overlooking the Square there is a plaque to commemorate this. The School closed for lessons on 25 April 1947, but the Richards Trust is still very much in operation today. It now helps the under-25s with the cost of further education.

The location of the original doors and windows to the schoolhouse can still be seen on the wall that runs from the butcher's shop to the bus shelter. The entrance would have been behind what is now the back wall of the current bus shelter. The school's playground was behind the war memorial, on the opposite side of the road, known today as 'The Little Rec.', although the older people of the village who went to the school remember it as Higher Yard. The younger children played at the back of the school, which was known as the Lower Yard, now the site of the Legion's skittle alley. On the roof of the building the school bell still hangs, and this would have been used to call the children to school in the morning, and after dinner.

The war memorial was erected in 1920 to commemorate the 39 men from Silverton killed in the First World War. A further ten names were added in respect to those from the village who perished during the Second World War.

The small building that still stands at the other end of the wall to the war memorial was the fire station, housing the Silverton fire engine. This was a horse-drawn contraption, purchased in 1837 and typical of its period, basically a pump with a long handle on each side, which required no less than 22 men to operate it!

The building now used as a newsagency has been the site of a shop since the late 1800s, as has the butcher's shop next door. On the wall outside the butcher's shop is a cabinet where the minutes of Silverton Parish Council meetings and other local notices are displayed. In most villages in this country it is standard practice to have such notices displayed to allow parishioners to keep abreast of what is happening in their village. In this age of technology it is also possible for such notices to be made available on the Internet, offering them to a worldwide audience. Silverton has kept up with this technology and has its own website, the address for which is http://www.eclipse.co.uk/silverton/.

The shop on the corner of Tiverton Road, currently a Londis store, was owned for much of the 20th century by the Perratt family. Everything was sold here, from butter to barbed wire, from shotgun cartridges to wool and fabrics. Over the years, the shop has been an integral and vital part of village life. Transport was not available to the extent that it is today, and the needs of villagers had to be catered for within the parish as far as was possible. A walk around any village even 50 years ago would have shown several shops of all descriptions, and it was not uncommon for a village the size of Silverton to have two or more of the same trade - be it butcher, baker, or general store. As this walk progresses it will be seen that Silverton was a village with many shops.

Before leaving the Square, it is of interest to note that until the last quarter of the 19th century the village stocks were still to be seen to the right of the path that leads from the Square to the churchyard. Records show that they were last used in about 1850.

Top: *The dedication of the war memorial c.1920.*
Above: *Two cars parked outside Perratt's shop, early 1930s.*
Below: *The Square as seen from the Church tower.*

Ayshford's Garage in the mid 1930s with Ted Ayshford and his father Frank.

By-election in June 1923. Colonel Gilbert Troyte, the cousin of Francis Acland, was chosen by the Conservative Party as their candidate. Francis Acland was elected as Liberal MP for the Constituency. The General Election was held in November of the same year, and Francis was successful again but by a mere three votes.

Main picture: *The Square taken from Newcourt Road. The property now known as Old Church House Gallery is looking in need of repair.*
Top inset: *The window in the Old Church House overlooking Fore Street.*
Left: *Fire insurance plaque of the Phoenix Insurance Company.*

FORE STREET

Entering Fore Street, it is readily apparent that the scene has not changed very much over the last century. The Old Church House Gallery, on the left, was a butcher's shop at the start of the last century. When the butchery closed, the shop reverted to being a part of the house. However, in 1982, it became the present Gallery and was renovated to the state in which it would have stood many years ago. On the wall of the Gallery is a fire insurance plaque, one of two in Fore Street. It is, however, only a copy, as these plaques are highly collectable items and for that reason the original is kept elsewhere. Many years ago insurance companies would insure properties against fire, and place their company plaque on the wall of the insured house. In the unfortunate event of a fire at the property, only the fire-tender belonging to, or authorised by, that company would attend. There could well have been another company's tender close by, but it would only be used if the wall plaque was that of the company concerned!

The most obvious feature in Fore Street is the leat of constantly flowing water that runs from the High Street until it finally disappears under the road close to the Square. This water still flowed during the drought of 1976.

The thatched houses on the right are 14th-century hall houses. The chimney stacks are visible on the outside walls of the houses, as opposed to being part of the internal structure. The reason for this is that they were added some years after the properties were constructed. Originally there would have been no upper storey, each house being one or two large rooms. Fires were lit on the ground, often in the centre of the room, and the smoke would escape by means of a hole in the roof. The blackened roof timbers of these houses are still there to this day, although now located in what we term the lofts. When, in later years upper storeys were constructed, fires were lit in hearths set in an outside wall, and chimneys put on the outside to carry the smoke away from the house.

The Post Office has, in past years, been located in two of the houses in this terrace, numbers 2 and 4. The shop at the other end of the row now known as 'Cabbages and Kings' was at one time a saddlery, owned by a Mr Jennings.

Moving further up Fore Street, on the left is the Silverton Inn, which until recently had for generations been known as 'The New Inn'. The building has three floors. Various itinerant travellers, including drovers who would drive their sheep to market through the village, used the top floor as overnight

Left: *Fore Street. The car is a 1928 Morris Oxford Tourer, owned by Mr Ralph Bowerman from 1938. The Post Office is on the right of the picture in one of its various Fore Street locations.*

Above: *Ladies outside the Old Post Office, early 1900s. Note the irregular pavement.*

Above: *The old Fore Street Post Office, advertising Mortimer's Plymouth Dye Works.*

Right: *Taken in the 1960s, this photograph shows the hall houses, the first on the right being the original Post Office.*

Far right: *The old Fore Street Post Office again - this time with with a chocolate machine outside as well as a sign advertising the use of the telephone.*

Right: *Fore Street with the New Inn on the left and Jennings the saddlers on the right, c.1912.*

Below: *A view of Fore Street in the 1960s, from Willow Cottage (Redgates), showing Silverton House, the residence of Dr Hederman, and adjacent cottages.*

Left: *Fore Street with the Frost's butcher's shop on the left and Wisteria House (also below) on the right.*

Bottom right: *Charles Frost's bakery.*

Above: *Painting by Miss Laetitia Ward. The Skinners occupied the cottage on the near right. Albert came from this family of thatchers, and his work can be seen on many older village properties. He also thatched hay and corn ricks or stacks. However, should the hounds be heard, he would disappear, for he would have dropped everything to follow the hunt!*

Dawe's sweet shop in Fore Street. Mr Frost, the baker, with a barrel of cider in the background.

Fore Street still with the oil lamps. Archie Tremlett, the local blacksmith, has parked his bike outside his cottage as usual.

A 1930s view of Fore Street towards the Lamb Inn. Mr George Frost's butcher's shop is on the right.

A view of Fore Street with the Lamb Inn - prior to the building of the Methodist chapel.

❀ Fore Street Trade ❀

Ayshford's garage in the foreground. Notice the petrol pumps that were operated by hand. The street was decorated with flags and bunting possibly for George V's Jubilee in 1936.

Edward (Ted) Ayshford with sons Francis and James, and mechanic Dave Stenner, having returned from Exeter with a large girder mounted on the chassis of a partially dismantled Morris. This was towed behind his Austin Seven 'Bonzo' with Dave (the mechanic) standing on the chassis, steering the Morris and working the brakes!

accommodation. A lease dated 18 September 1824, includes the stipulation that the innkeeper, Mr James Courtney, pay the owner, Mr Benjamin Thomas, maltster, a yearly rent of £19.15s.0d. (£19-75). A further requirement was for him to 'repair and keep repaired the glass part of the windows', and to purchase:

... at a fair market price all the malt which he may have occasion to use in the brewing and making of beer and other malt liquor on the premises provided the lessor shall sell malt of a good and fair quality and that the lessee shall occupy and keep open the said premises as a Common Inn or Alehouse.

The building adjoining the New Inn was the coach house, and when it was converted to a private residence it was given that name.

Election Day, 23 June 1923.

The next property on the left was owned by one of the village blacksmiths, who was also a wheelwright. The abundance of working horses prior to the 20th century required the attentions of several blacksmiths, who in those days combined the art of forging metal with the day-to-day requirements of a farrier. The premises later changed to a garage selling petrol following the development of the automobile. A taxi service and car repair business grew, although in the early part of the last century there were but a handful of motor cars in the village. Above the old shop window the names of the owners would have been sign-written, and doubtless if the layers of paint could be removed the names of previous owners West, Gibbs and Ayshford would be revealed. The petrol pumps were to the left of the iron gates that now have 'Bill and Pen' written within them, the trading name of the now defunct private gym that was on the site until recently.

Opposite is, at the time of writing, a vacant site. Here the Audit Room once stood, with the New Hall at the rear. For many years this was the heart of the village, where all the important functions took place including dances, concerts, meetings, wedding receptions, auctions, and jumble sales. Constructed by Messrs Bradbeer & Sons of Willand, from plans drawn up by Exeter architect W.F.R. Ham Esq., the New Hall was built to the rear of the former Audit Room. The MP for Tiverton, Sir Francis Acland of Killerton House, officially opened it on 1 June 1932. In his speech, Sir Francis remarked on the spirit of the village that had resulted in the majority of the

necessary cash being raised. This was boosted by a loan made available by Mr Frankpitt, a businessman who lived in the village. That evening, celebrations commenced at 7.30p.m. with a whist drive, followed by a dance which continued until after 10p.m.

Used for various functions during the next 55 years, the building was declared unsafe by a surveyor, and during January 1990 was demolished. The property next to this site, number 18, was a bootmaker's shop run by Mr Thomas Bowerman. During the time of the construction of the Exe Valley railway line, Mr Bowerman would have enjoyed much trade mending the boots of the labourers involved in constructing that line.

The terraced red-brick houses on the opposite side of the road are Victorian. The first, No. 9, had its roof blown off in the severe storms of 1990, and the two chimneys fell through the roof, landing on the beds. Fortunately no one was injured. It had been a general store and greengrocery run by Mrs Edith Bowerman for 20 years. These houses were constructed to replace the original buildings on the site, destroyed in one of Silverton's disastrous fires. It is interesting to note that the original deeds of No. 9 show it as 'The Ring Of Bells', being the site of an old public house. A lease dated 8 June 1816, to be found in the Devon Record Office, between Mr Richard Mortimore of Cullompton, Gentleman, and Mr Benjamin Thomas of Silverton, Maltster (the same gentleman that owned the New Inn), shows that a rent of £8 was charged for the establishment. This was payable by four equal payments in the year viz. Midsummer Day, Michaelmas Day, Christmas Day and Lady Day, and also included a clause instructing that the premises be 'plastered and whitewashed when and as often as shall be necessary', and that they be kept in 'good substantial and tenable repair'.

On the other end of the red-brick terrace houses can be seen the frontage of a former shop. During the middle of the last century it was a sweet shop, owned by the Dawe sisters, Sarah Ann (Annie) and Ivis. Later it was the Post Office but reverted to a private residence in 1979.

Directly opposite is the current Post Office. Prior to being such it was one of the village's many butcher's shops, owned at one time by the Western family. The thatched house to the left is Ivy Cottage. Some years ago, when repair work was being carried out, a book was found hidden in the walls – an Almanac

Top right: *The Dymond family outside their home, the Old Dairy - now the site of the footpath leading to the Health Centre and Millennium Hall.*

Above: *Walter Marsh, landlord of the Lamb Inn, with three customers including (third from the left) Vernon Valentine and (far right) Mr J.B. French.*

Above right: *Albert Skinner, thatcher, at Stockwell Cottage in August 1966 on his last thatching assignment.*

Above: *An early-20th century photograph of children in Fore Street. Note the cobbled footpath.*

Left: *Mr and Mrs Yeo outside their shop in Fore Street, where a variety of goods, including sweets were sold.*

Above: *The demolition of the Audit Room and New Hall in 1990. The operator of this machine stated that the building was the most solid one he had ever demolished!* (G.J.H. Parnell)

Left: *Scaffolding around the New Hall prior to demolition.* (J. Tree)

containing details of kings and queens, weights and measures, market days, etc., and printed in 1584.

There is a lane to the left of Ivy Cottage which still has a postal address of Fore Street, even though it branches off from the main street and leads to the doctor's surgery, the car park and also the new Millennium Hall. In this lane is a house called The Old Dairy, from where a herd of cows belonging to Mr and Mrs Cecil Hutchings travelled to the fields now occupied by Silverdale.

As the main street bends slightly to the left, on the right hand side of the road can be seen Bakers Cottage, which, as the name suggests, was one of the bakeries serving the village. It was owned by a Mr Charles Frost, who also owned the house to the right of it. This property is the site of the old pound, where a horse-powered machine crushed apples from the many local orchards, to make real Devon cider. The windows of that house are fairly new, a fact which is verified by early photographs that show the property with none.

Years ago 'gentlemen of the road', or tramps as they are more commonly known, would walk out from Exeter and stop here to enjoy a hunk of bread and cheese, more than likely washed down with a mug of the locally-brewed cider. They would then carry on their walk to Tiverton, returning to Exeter the following day, and stopping here once again. Mr

Frost also had a coalyard situated to the rear of these properties.

The thatched cottages opposite are set back from the road. There is evidence in the roof space of an additional wall being built to increase the width of these properties, and the necessary larger thatched roof being built over the previous thatch.

The large thatched house adjoining the cottages (with the porch at the front) is Silverton House. From 1912 it was the home of Dr Clayton Jones and his successor, Dr Hederman, who carried on the practice for forty years, from 1927 until 1967. The door on the left led into the small waiting room, but when this was full the patients would spill out on to the street. Dr Hederman was also a much-respected person in the village, and after his death the Parish Council decided that in recognition of all his work, a road would be named in his memory – Hederman Close.

Next to the door of the former waiting room can be seen the remains of what was one of the village taps supplying water to the people of Fore Street and High Street. At the start of the 20th century, properties in Silverton were not connected to a public mains supply, as this method did not arrive in Silverton until 1939. The Parish Council was obliged to closely monitor the water usage, and this would be much to the annoyance of the women of the village who frequently carried out their weekly laundry on the same day.

No. 42 Fore Street is a brick-built property known as Fursdon House, which at one time was one of the various locations of the village Police Station. The name 'Fursdon' has appeared in parish documents for centuries, and relates to the various members of the family of that name who still occupy Fursdon House between Cadbury and Thorverton. A

Above: *Fore Street showing the former New Inn in 2000.* (J. Tree)

Below: *Fore Street showing Cleeve Cottage. It is interesting to note that in 2000 a telephone cable is attached to almost every property, whereas the 1930* Kelly's Directory *lists only six in the whole village! Dr. Patrick Hederman, Physician, No. 3; George Short, Builder, 5; Robert Wellington, Farmer at Worth, 6; Charles Medland, Farmer at Poundsland, 7; Edward Ayshford, Cycle repairer, 8; and Perratt & Co., Grocer, 9.* (J. Tree)

Top right: *The leat flowing at the edge of The High Street.* (J. Tree)

Above: *Recent view of Fore Street from Willow Cottage.* (J. Tree)

property named 'Fursdon' is the subject of an indenture dated 3 September 1816 held at the Devon Record Office, between William Martin of Holcombe Regis, a yeoman, and William Courtenay of Silverton, a baker. Also at an auction at the Rougemont Hotel, Exeter, on Friday 21 November 1919 there was offered for sale:

... smallholding viz: all that valuable property known as Fursdons, comprising of dwelling house, and shop (formerly two houses) with a frontage to Fore Street and containing seven bed-rooms, shop, dairy, 2 front and 2 back kitchens. At the rear are brick and stone built slaughter house and stable with loft over, large cow shed, lean to calves house, brick built and slated 4 division piggery and meal house. There is a small orchard and excellent close of meadow land (no. 481 on ordnance survey map) now let to Mr. W. Pridham. (Possession can be had at Michaelmas 1920.)

From this it would appear that Fursdon was the previous name of the property now known as 'Willow Cottage', but until the 1970s as 'Redgates'.

It was here that in the 1930s a farm, slaughterhouse and butchery was owned by George Frost. The butcher's shop has long since gone, but ran from the left of the property towards the road edge.

Opposite are three cottages. One of these known as 'The Spragues' was once a sweet shop, next to which is 'Wisteria House', and adjoining this are Manor Cottages, with another fire plaque on the wall.

Until very recently there was a dairy and general store to the left side of Fore Street, just before the Lamb Inn. Indeed, at the time of publication it laid the sad claim to being the last shop to close in Silverton. Prior to being a dairy, it had at one time been the baker's shop, owned by Charlie Dymond. The old bread oven is still inside the building, although not now visible. From the Lamb Inn, the view looking towards the High Street is the scene painted by Reverend Ward's daughter Laetitia, at the end of the 19th century. The tall wall on the right of her picture has gone and the Methodist Chapel has since been built on the site.

At various times over the past century there have been at least 17 shops and businesses operating throughout the length of Fore Street.

Looking down Fore Street from Ingleside, c.1920.

Main picture: *Fore Street in the 1920s. Ivy Cottage is on the right, with a sign advertising that the occupier is J.T. (John Thomas) Baal, Boot and Shoe Maker.*
Insets: *Leather-bound book found in Ivy Cottage, dated 1584 and page from the book.*

Main picture: *Rose Cottage and courtyard, situated behind Fore Street hall houses.*
Inset: *An infant's shoe, dating from the 16th Century, was found in one of the cottages at the top of the High Street.*

HIGH STREET

The brick houses on the left of High Street, Cotton's Row, looking up the hill, were rebuilt in 1902, and a plaque on the gable end commemorates this date, together with the initials and crest of Edward Cotton (rector from 1660–75). The Silverton Parochial Trust built these on the site of the former Cottons Court, where the workhouse was situated (which burnt down on 29 July 1900). The house next door, Charity Cottage, was saved with a minimum amount of damage. The Bishop Cotton Charity owned this property, along with Cottons Court. On the south-facing wall of the red-brick Charity Cottages, children have over the years carved their names into the brick-work and these are still visible today. Opposite is Omega Cottage, which was a general store until the 1970s, when Mr and Mrs James French owned it.

On the left of the street is a row of terraced cottages, which were built in 1842. In common with all properties occupied by working-class families, these were small by modern standards, with two rooms on each floor. In 1925 the Silverton Paper Mill purchased most of these for the use of their workers. In the 1970s they were sold by the mill and modernised, including the addition of porches at the front. They are now pleasant, individually owned, sought-after properties, and despite being no longer connected to the former mill, they are still known locally as 'the Mill Cottages'.

Above right: *The late Bill Gooding delivering to Mill Cottages in the High Street, c.1980.*

Right: *Mill Cottages in 2000.*

Below: *Silverton High Street in the late 1800s.*

At the top of the street is High Bullen. The name is a corruption of High-Bull-Ring which implies that Silverton was important enough to have two bull rings – the lower and higher. The Bullring was the place where bulls were baited – a process which was said to tenderise the meat.

The cottages on the right originally comprised three sections – the weaver's cottage, the workshop and the wool store. Some years ago an infant's shoe, thought to date from the 16th century, was found in

This was taken outside Charity Cottages c.1920. The lady with the pram is Mrs French, who owned the shop opposite. Also here are twin boys Ralph and Bert Andrews (born in April 1912); babe in arms is Bessie Selley with her grandmother. The lady in the door at the rear is Mrs Gillian Andrews.

Main picture: *High Street and Charity Cottages, 2000.*
Inset: *Date plaque on Charity Cottages.*

Mrs Mary (Polly) French in the doorway of the shop with her daughter Sybil c.1926.

Mary French outside her shop in the High Street, c.1932, with her grandson, Derek.

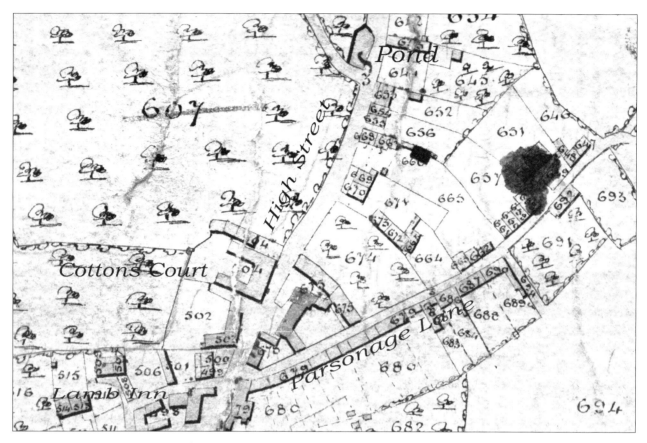

Tithe map showing High Street and Parsonage Lane.

the roof. A mummified cat was also found in the property, and it is thought that this would have been put there in an attempt to ward off evil spirits.

Opposite these cottages is a seat on the area known as the Pond site. This was the site of the Fire Service Pond, required to store water for the fire engine. It was developed from a spring and road-side swamp, the site being excavated, and a brick wall built on the north and south sides. The wall that was constructed on the east side adjacent to the High Street was some two feet thick and five to six high, enabling a store of water four feet deep against the north wall, and a depth of eight to ten feet at the south end. Water control was by a wheel and worm operating a locked door. The water could be increased from two ponds further up the hillside, where water could be released via a sluice gate when necessary, allowing water to wash down the road, so filling the pond at the bottom of the hill – basic, but no doubt very efficient for that period!

At the bungalow above No. 36 High Street two chimney pots can be seen being used for flower displays. These are relics from Silverton Park, the ornate mansion of Lord Egremont described on page 65.

Continuing up the hill will take the walker into Old Butterleigh Road, once the stagecoach route between Silverton and Tiverton. It is difficult to imagine how it would have been possible for a team of horses to pull a loaded stage up such a hill that only

has one short stretch of flat road. Equally as difficult must have been the journey down the same hill.

At the top of the hill is Christ Cross, known locally as Criss Cross. The views from here offer a magnificent panorama in all directions. To the north-east on a clear day can be seen the Wellington Monument, whilst to the east Sidmouth Gap is clearly visible. To the south is the Exe Estuary, where the River Exe ends its long, meandering journey from Exmoor, having passed very close to the village on its way to the sea.

Before the hill starts its rise to Criss Cross the road on the left leads to Silverdale Park, an estate of 49 bungalows built in the late 1960s. At the top of the short climb, a lane goes off to the right where there are some farm buildings and a field called Pigs Park. Here is Fordton Lane, leading to a public footpath that crosses Pigs Park and goes to the top of the hill from where it is possible to obtain a beautiful view of the village and beyond, with Killerton in the background. The path carries on towards a prehistoric enclosure and then on into the Burn Valley.

Continuing down through Silverdale Park, it becomes Applemead, a mixture of late-1960s houses and bungalows that were built on former orchards, which in common with thousands in England have given way to development. These were known as Shute and Dry Close Orchard, and would have produced much fruit and spectacular spring colour.

Tiverton Road

At the bottom of Applemead is Tiverton Road, which passes Great Pitt Farm, once the mansion of the Land family, where it is recorded that ornamental ceilings, destroyed when the property was rebuilt many years ago, depicted the rural scenes of stag hunting and of fishing.

After this the road rises and then dips again, before joining the main Exeter to Tiverton road at 'Jenny's Portion', said to be named after a girl who had the good fortune to inherit land there in a will. Here also can be found the field known as Shobrooks Close, where sheep were kept while the drovers lodged in the village over night.

Retracing the same route will return the walker to the village, past some extremely old thatched cottages on the left that appear on the parish tithe map, as do the houses immediately after King Street. Huntley Lodge was shown on this document as a barn, but has since been converted into a house. The house at the rear, Briar Cottage, is all that now remains of a row of cottages that was destroyed by yet another village fire in the 19th century. A short distance further on will be found Pembridge Cottage, and the large house next door named Wayside, which once rejoiced under the rather inauspicious name of Coggins Tenements!

The stream that runs down High Street and Fore Street continues its travels along part of Tiverton Road where it goes underground and reappears in the garden of Wayside. It then continues down to the main road at the bottom of the steep valley where it joins the River Exe. There are still riparian rights to the water in this stream.

On the left side of the road can be found the site of Archie Tremlett's blacksmith's shop. He was the blacksmith and farrier for the village, carrying on his business there until the early 1970s. He was one of the old village characters, as was George Carpenter who had a barber's shop on the same site. George was disabled, but never let this affect his sense of humour.

Further up the road is Old Church Cottage. This was owned by the Revd Tripp, and was the home of his carriage driver. Prior to entering the Square, on the left at the rear of the Gallery, there is still a riding mount. These can often be found outside properties - especially farms - and would have been used by the owners as a means of mounting their horse.

Pitt Farm in the 1920s.

Left: *Tiverton Road with Wayside on the left and Archie Tremlett's smithy on the right. Note the high wall at the lower end of the road, with Pitt Farm in the distance, c.1930s.*

Below: *The barber's shop beside the smithy in Tiverton Road.* (P. Crabtree)

Right: *George Carpenter, a well-known hairdresser. His barber's shop sign was carved by local craftsman Jack Perrin.*

Far right: *George Carpenter on his premises, where he also sold a wide range of toiletries.*

Below: *First view of the village when approached from Jenny's Portion.*

KING STREET

A very narrow, interesting part of the village, King Street is located in one of the older parts of the parish. At the start of the 20th century, many of the houses had no floorboards, the floor being earth covered with whatever the individual householders could afford. Some would have had rush matting, some stone slabs, and others merely compacted soil.

In line with many other traditional Devon villages, Silverton was originally constructed with one main street – in this case it was called Fore Street. Here those people of importance and wealth would have lived. There would be 'back lanes' going off the main street where servants, agricultural labourers, etc. lived. Back Lane had its name changed to King Street in the late-19th century, and in the words of a Devon proverb – 'Us can't all live in Vore Street so there was a Back Lane for the rest of us'.

Further up King Street, on the left, stands a row of old terraced cottages. There were also some more cottages further up the road (where the old people's bungalows now stand), but due to their dilapidated condition they were considered uninhabitable and were demolished. On the right of the street will be found a house called Westerlands, which was another location for the village Police Station.

King Street was also the rear entrance to the former dairy in Fore Street, and it was from here that the battery-powered milk floats would leave early each morning, laden with bottles of milk, orange juice, cream and other goods. Not only did they serve Silverton, but also other villages such as Broadclyst and Stoke Canon. The journey home would have been very slow, as the batteries would have lost much of their power during the morning round.

At the top end of King Street stands the Lamb Inn, at the junction with Fore Street.

Top: *Thomas Knowles, rabbit catcher, at his cottage in Back Lane (King Street).*

Right: *One of the two taps in King Street, at one time the only water supply there.*

PARSONAGE LANE

As the name suggests, this lane once led to the former parsonage of the village. On the right is the Methodist Chapel. Opened in 1914, it replaced an older chapel situated on the crest of the hill now the site of two semi-detached houses.

The next building on the right is the former Police House, the last building to be used for this purpose in the village. The terrace of cob cottages known as The Court once continued to the junction with Fore Street, until destroyed by fire in April 1878.

The lane then descends and on the right can be seen a cob and stone wall, all that remains of a long-vanished property. Where Parsonage Lane ends a footpath continues which is known as the Mead Path. On the left of this footpath are two ponds, thought to be the medieval stew ponds of the old Parsonage, dating from the 13th century. The ponds would have been stocked with fish to supply the property with fish for Fridays, vigils and the 40 days of lent.

At the top is the entrance to the former Parsonage (the Old Rectory). In 1937 it was sold by the Church, and the new owners re-named it Prispen House (derived from Priests Pen). Unfortunately, this fine house was destroyed by fire in 1990, and a new housing estate has recently been built on the area, named Prispen View to commemorate the former property.

Prispen House from Parsonage Lane.

A view of Lily Lake taken in the 1930s. The lorry in front of the four houses on the left of the picture belonged to Mr Arthur Pyne, a coal merchant from Hele.

COACH ROAD

Adjacent to Prispen View is Roach Lane, which leads to a public footpath that eventually reaches Criss Cross, mentioned earlier. The present Silverton School was built in 1975, to replace separate buildings in the village for boys and girls. Opposite the school is Wyndham Road, an estate developed since the 1970s, named after the Wyndham family who were lords of the manor of Silverton for many years. Two roads that adjoin this have links with Silverton history: French Close (named after George French who was clerk to the Parish Council for many years), and Davies Close (named after Edward Davies, former Fire Chief of the Silverton Brigade).

Also in Coach Road is one of the entrances to the Recreation Ground, which has a football pitch and children's play area. Here can be seen a massive oak tree which is thought to be 1000 years old and which in recent years has become the village symbol.

The triangle of land formed between Coach Road, Park Road and the footpath to Park Close was purchased by the then Tiverton Rural District Council from the Church Commissioners in 1926. The sum of £300 was agreed for this, on the condition that it was to be used for the 'erection of houses for the persons of the working class'. Almost 75 years later, a term such as this in a contract would not be considered 'politically correct'!

To the east of this area is 'Heal Eye Stream', which was thought to have healing powers, and it is said that people came from miles around to visit this stream. This part of the village was known as Lily Lake, where it is said that pilgrims came to wash themselves lily-white.

At the junction of Coach Road and School Road, are two domestic properties that have been converted from the former school for girls, built here in 1847. This became co-educational in 1947 until it finally closed in 1975. An interesting plaque is still visible above the main door (see page 95).

Top: *The Girls' School, now converted into dwellings.*
Above: *Coach Road in 1879 – a painting looking from the entrance of Prispen House, initialled by M.B.H.*
(Painting loaned by Colin Selley)

Above: *Central Garage in the 1930s, when owned by Fred Glanville. Two known people are on the left - Bill Carpenter senr and, to his left, Bill Webber.*

Left: *The Devon Fire Brigade fighting the fire at Central Garage.* (Barry Park)

Bottom: *The Civil War sword said to have been found in a hedge at Christ Cross.*

Opposite top: *Tree planting ceremony in The Berry, with Revd Heathcote officiating aided by his wife (with the spade) and Mr Faraday (with the Homburg hat).*

SCHOOL ROAD

School Road leads back to the Square where this walk commenced. The name has not altered despite the school being relocated, but for some unknown reason it was previously called Welch Road. Two Victorian cottages half way up the road, on the right, are called Welch Cottages. Opposite the Evangelical Church is Newcourt Cottage, formally known as Butts Cottage.

During the Civil War the Parliamentary army travelled towards Exeter. It is recorded in *The Parliamentary Army in the Civil War* by Joshua Sprigg(e) that at Silverton on 20 October 1645 a Council of War was called to decide 'whether to advance further west before Exeter was reduced, or to march up to the enemy and relieve Plymouth.'

The Royalists held Exeter throughout that winter, and on 30 March 1646 it is said that Silverton was made the temporary headquarters of the Parliamentary Army of some 5000 men, under the command of Sir Thomas Fairfax. They are thought to have camped in the fields adjoining School Road.

St Mary's is the newest estate in the village, and is still under construction at the time of writing. It is built on the site of the last of two garages in Silverton, Central Garage. A disastrous fire on 29 February, 1990 nearly cost Don Brady the proprietor his life, when fumes from the petrol tank of the car that was being repaired exploded.

CHURCH ROAD

Most of the houses in the road are comparatively new, including a development by Wimpey Homes, built in the early 1980s named Hederman Close after the late village doctor. Where Church Road meets The Berry is Nettleworth House, previously known as Berry Villa. In the 19th century this was a private school, and in 1915 the house, part of the Silverton Estate, was sold at auction for £600.

On the left is New Barn Lane, which leads in the direction of Silverton Paper Mill. Although this road does not go directly to the mill, many workers would have used this route on their daily journey to work from the village, and followed the footpath over the fields, beside the River Culm. It is still an interesting walk today as the area abounds with fascinating wildlife, including kingfishers, swans and the occasional otter. Care must be taken, however, as it is necessary to cross the main Exeter to London railway line.

On one side of New Barn Lane is an old cobbled path with the inscription WD 1860, depicted in a different colour stone (*above right*). Hidden by weeds for many years, it has recently been uncovered. The road here would frequently flood in winter, and the high footpath was most probably built for the people using the path to remain dry.

As the road bends there is what remains of a cob wall. This once surrounded a house and barn

known as Berry Barn, which is listed on the tithe apportionment.

The short steep hill towards the church is lined by the avenue of lime trees planted in 1660 to commemorate the Restoration of the Monarchy. This area is known as The Berry (or Bury), and at the crest is the entrance to St Mary's Church.

The church clock on the west side of the tower overlooks the Square, and was bought with money given by the people of Silverton in 'God's Name', to commemorate the 60th year of Queen Victoria's reign in 1897.

The pavement running along Church Road is quite high in relation to the road itself. The first house on the right was the Rectory until 1991 when it was sold as private accommodation. Prior to this it was the Sexton's house. Next are two Georgian houses and then 'The Old Pound House' at the corner. The land opposite was once Balls Farm, which illustrates just how much the community has moved away from its agricultural roots; between the wars farm animals straying on the village roads would have been an everyday sight.

Berry Villa, c.1914.

Cottages on The Berry, photographed during the early part of the 20th century.

*A late-19th century photograph, taken at the junction of Church Road and New Barn Lane.
The group on the left are most probably from Berry Villa.*

Church Terrace viewed from The Berry, with The Three Tuns in the background.

Church Road, 2000.

The Three Tuns and cottages in Exeter Road, 2000. (J. Tree)

NEWCOURT ROAD

Church Road joins Newcourt Road. To the left before Channons Farm is a muddy lane that is shown on the tithe map to have been the site of several buildings in the 19th century. The gravel pit, just before the junction with Exeter Road, is where material would have been quarried for building. The road carries on down Kenson Hill, over Stumpy Cross, which is the junction with an ancient road from Crediton and the west, to Bristol and eastern England. Just before the parish boundary with Rewe is Dunsmore, where Princess Henrietta is said to have sought refuge during the Civil War.

Turning right from Church Road leads one back to the Square. Labourers working on the construction of the railway and main road to Tiverton in the 19th century are said to have stayed in the terraced houses situated on the right. It has also been known in the past as 'Navvies Row', 'Church Terrace' and 'Satchels Row'.

The narrow lane on the left is known as Balls Lane, and leads to Exeter Road. It contains a substantial Victorian house, which was formerly the schoolmaster's house.

EXETER ROAD

Exeter Road contains a terrace of thatched, cob cottages that end with The Three Tuns Inn. The village would have had many public houses or alehouses, some say up to a dozen, but it would have been necessary for the landlord to have had a second occupation; in the case of The Three Tuns, he was also a blacksmith. The earliest known record of The Three Tuns is an advertisement of a sale to be held there on Wednesday, 5 January 1791, although the building is thought to be much earlier.

Electricity for lighting was available at Silverton from 1928, when Christie Brothers installed a Rushton crude-oil cold-starter engine at Cockhayne, the white property on the right of the road. It was purely a local supply and the current was switched on between 5p.m. and 11p.m. This was superseded in the early 1930s when electricity to the village was supplied from Exeter.

Just past Cockhayne is a gateway to the Jubilee Field. This was named in commemoration of the Jubilee of George V and Queen Mary in 1935, when it was the site for the sports day. At this point, the road was closed during the Second World War as it was requisitioned by the 953rd Field Artillery Battalion of the US Army, which was temporarily stationed in the village. Their guns were kept in the road with camouflage netting over them. Older Silvertonians have clear memories of the American GIs being in the village, although one day when the village came to life, the Army had disappeared. It later transpired that this was, in fact, D-Day, and that they had dispersed to the various embarkation areas on the South Devon coast. Later in the war, the field was used to house prisoners of war captured in Europe.

Exeter Road; Symond's Farmhouse taken from the 1915 Silverton estate sale catalogue.

Newcourt Farm during the early 1900s.

This photograph was taken in 1933 outside the home of Mrs Carpenter senr from where the daily newspaper was distributed. The Carpenter family are off to a football match.

Old cottages and The Three Tuns Inn in Exeter Road with Mrs Jessie Carpenter and her children.

This is currently known as Church Terrace.
The occupants of these cottages were obviously keen to be in the photograph, early 1900s.

The Faraday fire in Exeter Road, 9 July 1934.

Chapter 3
Fires in Silverton

If any one influence has been most significant in the development of Silverton as we know today it has been fire. The cob-and-lath construction of the cottages, coupled with the thatched roofs, made for a highly flammable combination, and one which had long been noted in Exeter, where the use of thatch had been forbidden for at least two centuries from c.1700. The only means of heating and cooking was by naked flame – the major cause of the many disasters which occurred throughout the centuries. The red-brick cottages such as those owned by the Charity in High Street, are typical of many throughout the village that were built on the site of burnt cottages. The following reports from Trewman's *Exeter Flying Post* describe many of these fires:

Early photograph of the fire engine, with shafts for horse removed.

7th. April, 1814 *On Sunday last the grist mills [469 to 479 on tithe map] of Mr. Gale, of Silverton, caught fire, while the family were at Church, and with the dwelling house, great part of the furniture, and a quantity of corn were totally destroyed.*

19th. May, 1831 *On Friday forenoon last, while Mr. Francis Lee, his wife and others of his family, were attending the market in this City, a fire broke out at his house, Hayne Farm, in the Parish of Silverton. Every assistance was rendered from Hayne House and places adjacent, and through these exertions a considerable part of the furniture, wearing apparel etc. were preserved, but the dwelling house was entirely destroyed. Fortunately the wind blew the contrary direction from the other farm buildings, which (though in great danger from contiguity and fierceness of the blaze) were, from the judicious means resorted to by those present, preserved. It is not known how this misfortune occurred, but it is attributed to accident. We hear that Mr. Lee was uninsured.*

25th. May, 1837 *At half past nine o'clock in the morning of Thursday last (18th. May), a fire broke out in the town of Silverton, when an express was immediately sent to Exeter for assistance, and the West of England engines, with a full complement of men, at once left the smoking ruins of Paris Street and proceeded, with the utmost expedition, to Silverton, reaching the scene of devastation there, being a distance of seven miles, in twenty-five minutes. The houses being thatched, the flames had made considerable progress, and were not subdued until more than forty houses were in ruins, and a large number of families rendered houseless, much of their furniture and other property being destroyed. The rapidity of the flames was most terrific, and, but for the great exertions of the gentry, farmers and inhabitants of the neighbourhood, aided by the most efficient services of the firemen, the whole town must have been reduced to ashes. Sir Thomas Acland was present during the whole time of the fire, blending all the powers of his mind to the suggestion of the best mode of staying the progress of the destructive element, and exerting all his personal energies heedless of danger, in assisting to effect that object. The Rev. Mr. Barker, and several gentlemen and yeomanry, also rendered great service; and on the flames being subdued, a subscription was immediately raised for the temporary relief of the sufferers. The only material accident that occurred, was the falling of a cob wall, by which an aged woman named Thomas, had her leg fractured, and received other injury. She was immediately taken to the Devon and Exeter Hospital, where we regret to add, she has since died of her injuries.*

A meeting of the Parishioners was held in the Church in the afternoon, the Rev. Mr. Barker in the chair, for the purpose of adopting modes of relief and of providing for the immediate protection of the poorer sufferers. A committee was appointed, consisting of the Rev. Mr. Barker, Col. Glover, Mr. W. U. Tripp, Mr. Mortimore, Mr. Dewdney, Mr. J. Gould, Mr. Hewitt, Mr. Cutliffe, Mr. Aplin, Mr. Braddick, the Churchwardens and Overseers, Mr. Brice and Mr. Player, five of whom are to be a quorum for the management of the fund, which was immediately commenced by the subscriptions which follow.

The charity and benevolence of the public is, on behalf of the sufferers, respectfully solicited by the committee, who with confidence that the present is a case deserving the attention of all who are charitably disposed, will thankfully receive subscriptions, which will also be received at the various Banks in Exeter. Mr. Thomas Dewdney was requested to act as Treasurer.

A sum in excess of £260 was collected from sympathisers including almost ten pounds from the people of Thorverton.

INCENDIARISM Within a short time of the West of England engines had left Silverton on Thursday afternoon for Exeter, intelligence arrived that a fire had broken out at Hayne Farm (and not at Hayne House as reported by a contemporary) the residence of Mr. Elworthy, about one mile from that place. One of the West of England engines from Thorverton, together with an engine belonging to Mr. Matthews of Rewe Mills, which remained at Silverton to watch the subdued flames there, were immediately despatched to the scene of the fire; and a messenger was sent after the engines that had proceeded for Exeter, but did not get up to them till after they had arrived in this City, when one of them immediately returned, and with the exertions of the firemen, to whom great praise is due succeeded in extinguishing it. A barn and pound-house were destroyed, and we regret to state that, from the position of the fire when discovered, and the situation of these buildings, the general belief is that this conflagration was the diabolical act of an incendiary. Every exertion is making to discover the perpetrator of the crime.

Yesterday (Tuesday) morning, soon after six o'clock, it was discovered that the pound-house of Mrs. Webber snr. in Silverton, was on fire. A messenger was despatched to Thorverton, and the engine from that town promptly brought to the spot: and we are happy to add that the fire was got under without material damage.

On Saturday morning another instance of calamity from fire occurred at Burnhayes Farm, in the Parish of Bickleigh, about two miles from Silverton, and in the occupation of Mr. Samuel Tremlett. The flames were first discovered issuing from the outhouses, and before their progress could be arrested, the whole of these, about 30 hogsheads of cider, and 50 empty hogsheads, with sundry implements of husbandry, were totally destroyed. Fortunately the fire did not extend the farmhouse, but we regret to say that there is some reason to suppose it is the work of an incendiary. Strict enquiries are making as to the origin both of this and of the fire at Hayne Farm, but up to this morning, however, no individual has been apprehended on suspicion of being concerned in the villainous act.

29th. June, 1837 It is with the deepest regret that we record another instance of calamity of this kind in this Parish, a linhay at Ash, the residence of Mr. Braddick, being about a quarter before 6 o'clock, on the morning of Thursday last discovered to be on fire. Prompt assistance was immediately afforded, and a small engine which has been kept in the Town since the late fires, until a more powerful one is ready, was drawn to the spot, and proved of the most essential service. The engine at Thorverton also, was again speedily brought to the assistance of their distressed neighbours, and likewise greatly contributed to continuing the space of the conflagration. To this end also the attention of the persons present was judiciously directed, the linhay communicating at one end with the barn, and the other with a range of stabling, and thus with the dwelling house. As well right and left then, through the arduous exertions of many persons, the communication was cut off, and these ranges of buildings preserved, but the linhay was entirely destroyed. The origin of the fire is at present unknown, but from the circumstances of time and place, there is but too much reason to fear that it was wilful, the work is incendiary.

26th. January, 1849 A fire broke out about eight o'clock on the morning of the 26th. inst. at Silverton, on a farm called Youlton, belonging to the representatives of the late Lord Egremont and Lord Ilchester, near the village and occupied by Mr. White, but by the praiseworthy exertions of the inhabitants and engine men of Silverton, who immediately brought their engine into work, the fire was prevented extending further than the building in which it originated, and those under the same roof. The alarm soon spread, and within half an hour after the express left Silverton, Mr. Row, the agent of the West of England Insurance Company at Thorverton, with their engine was on the spot. A pound house and cellars with some outbuildings, were totally destroyed and the dwelling house was saved from the thatch being stripped off. The premises are not insured, but the furniture and farming stock, belonging to Mr. White are insured in the West of England Office. The fire is supposed to have been caused from some hot ashes being taken from the fire place in the morning and put in the outbuildings where the ashes were usually kept.

17th. November, 1859   On Thursday night last a fire broke out in this town, and two dwelling houses the property of Mr. John Nick of Silverton, Farmer, were destroyed. The Silverton fire-engine was speedily in attendance. The property is insured.

26th. August, 1874   Waterslave Farm House, Silverton, the property of Mrs. Webber, was entirely destroyed by fire on Sunday.

10th. April, 1878   The inhabitants of the pleasantly situated and usually quiet village of Silverton were greatly alarmed by a fire which broke out about noon on Sunday, and spread with such rapidity that before it could be extinguished sixteen houses were destroyed, and the occupants to the number of about sixty, found themselves homeless and well nigh destitute.

The fire originated in the chimney of a cottage at the head of Parsonage Lane, occupied by a labourer named William Davey, and was first discovered soon after noon, just as people were leaving Church. Parsonage Lane is a narrow thoroughfare branching off the main road at the north end of the village, and most of the houses in it were very old and inflammable, being built for the most part of cob and covered with thatch. These cottages were, with one or two exceptions, occupied by labourers and old people past work.

Prompt measures were taken to extinguish the chimney and there the damage would probably have ended had it not been for the high wind, which carried flakes of burning soot onto the thatched roofs adjoining, and quickly set two or three of the dwellings in a blaze. A man named Gosling, who lived just opposite, was about to sit down to dinner with his family when the alarm was raised, and almost before he had time to look around the whole cottage was wrapped in flame. In a few minutes the local engine, under the direction of Mr. Loaring, was on the spot, and shortly afterwards the engines from Bradninch and Thorverton arrived. The power thus brought to bear was however found to be quite insufficient to master the flames, which spread from house to house with alarming rapidity, and accordingly a telegram was sent off to Exeter, via Thorverton, for more help. In less than an hour after receipt of the telegram one of the West of England engines,

under the command of Captain Honey, had been conveyed to Silverton - a distance of eight miles or more. The Sun engine, Captain Tucker, followed shortly afterwards.

By this time the fire had worked its way down Parsonage Lane, having obtained the mastery of the whole row of cottages, except one or two which had been partially saved by stripping the thatch, and another which had a tiled roof. The Exeter Brigade, seeing how matters were going, at once set to work to prevent the fire extending up and down the central thoroughfare and across it. The road is very narrow at the junction with Parsonage Lane, and, as many of the houses in the locality were thatched, the task of checking the progress of the flames was a very arduous one. The houses on the opposite side, including the Lamb Inn, caught fire readily; but the constant stream of water directed on these buildings from the several engines, seconded by the efforts of men armed with buckets, prevented the flames from obtaining a hold on them. Very fortunate indeed this was, for had the fire once obtained any headway in the central part of the village, the greater part of it must have gone. For a time a good supply of water was obtained from ponds in the neighbourhood, and though it was almost exhausted in a couple of hours, it lasted long enough to get the fire under. The roof of the Methodist Chapel, close by Gosling's house, at one time caught fire, but the building received no material injury. Cotton's row, at the end of the Lane a property of considerable value, given to the Parish by the late Dr. Cotton for the benefit of the poor, was placed in considerable jeopardy. Four times it caught fire, and was only saved from destruction by the watchfulness and activity of the Silverton and Thorverton firemen.

By four o'clock all apprehension of further danger was removed, and in a short time the fire was completely subdued. During the progress of the fire those of the neighbours who were not engaged in working the engines or fetching water, rendered valuable assistance to the unfortunate

THE STAR GRENADE FIRE EXTINGUISHER.

cottagers in removing the old and infirm to a place of safety, and saving their furniture and chattels. In one of the houses an old man named Thomas Courtenay had been invalided for years, and he had to be carried out on his bed. Ann Courtenay, between 80 and 90 years of age, who had lived in the same house for a great number of years, *obstinately refused to leave, but was gallantly rescued by P.C. Dameral, who rushed in through the blinding smoke, and brought her out just before the blazing roof fell in. Rev. H.F. Strangways was amongst the foremost in his exertions on behalf of his poor parishioners; Mrs. Strangways took charge of all the children, and*

sent them to the Rectory kitchen, where they received the kindest attention; the Misses Strangways and Miss. Kingsbury lent their assistance in fetching water to feed the engines, and in this work they soon found plenty of willing helpers. Mr. Passmore of the firm of Passmore and Savery, Exeter, deserves mention as prominent among visitors who rendered good service; while Mr. Webber, one of the leading laymen of Silverton, with Mr. Puddicombe, the village surgeon, likewise did all in their power to save goods, and in attending to the wants of the old and decrepit victims. Following is an approximate list of the families burnt out:- Davey, wife and four children; Vicary, wife and five children; Bolt, wife and three children; Thomas, wife and five children; Ann Courtenay, 87 years of age, and four or five old people over 70; King, wife and one child; John Andrews and Ann Andrews who occupied a cottage, their own property; Rew and two children; Gosling and two children. Excepting the cottages occupied by John and Ann Andrews, most of the cottages belonged to Messrs. Southcott and Barry, who were insured in the West of England and Sun Offices. Only one or two of the cottagers had insured their furniture, and those who were not left quite destitute have suffered considerable loss. Several of the burnt out families were lodged for the night at the Audit Room, where Dr. Puddicombe remained up to a late hour, doing what he could for the old and infirm.

During the day the scene of the fire was visited by hundreds of persons from the neighbourhood and from Exeter, and a subscription was started amongst them for the benefit of the sufferers.

28th. January, 1880   A fire broke out last Thursday morning on the premises of Ball's Farm, close to the Churchyard and in the occupation of Mr. G. Player. It appears that a farm lad had gone to the table with a lighted benzelene lamp, which he placed on the manger whilst attending to his duties, and a colt becoming restive the light was capsized into the rack, setting fire to the straw, and communicating to the building before the boy could extinguish the flames. The Silverton Fire Engine and Brigade under the instruction of Messrs. Loaring and Short, were soon on the spot and by their exertions the fire was subdued before much damage had been done, the only place burnt being the stable. The farm formed part of the property of the late Earl of Egremont, and the premises were insured in the Norwich Union Fire Office, but Mr. Player was uninsured.

6th. July, 1886   At the paper mills of Messrs. Hall and West, Silverton, yesterday, an explosion occurred whereby a man named John Hollett of Bradninch lost his life. One of the machines was stopped for the purpose of changing into another kind of paper, and the deceased went to turn off the steam from the drying cylinder. Instead of doing this he is supposed to have put on more pressure causing the cover of the cylinder to blow out with terrific force. Deceased was struck in the forehead, and the explosion forced out about twenty yards of the side of the building, which was of corrugated iron. Hollett was knocked into the River Culm, which he was immediately taken out insensible, and remained so until he died about two hours afterwards. Medical aid was summoned directly the accident occurred, and Messrs. Somer of Broadclyst, and Puddicombe of Silverton, were promptly in attendance, and remained with the man until he died.

28 September, 1886   Yesterday at the Cullompton Petty Sessions a man named Charles Cooksley, employed lately at the Bridge Paper Mills, was charged with setting fire to the dwelling house of Charles Webber, at Silverton on Saturday night. The evidence was to the effect that the house in question was a thatched one and the prisoner was seen strike a number of matches, get on some steps and raise the lights to the thatch. This took place about eleven o'clock at night, and was noticed by Mrs. Wagland, whose house is about fifty yards distant from Webber's. She drew the attention of Mr. H. Welland to what was going on, and the latter fetched P.C. Richards. When the Officer arrived prisoner was still striking matches and applying them to the thatch; but on hearing footsteps near he ran away. He, however, was soon caught by the policeman, and when the latter charged him, the only reply that he made was that he had not hurt anyone. Some matches and a piece of burnt paper which the constable found on the prisoner, also some burnt match stumps which he picked up, were produced in Court. It could not, Supt. Collins said, be ascertained that prisoner was prompted by any motive unless one of mischief. Mr. Read said prisoner had lived many years in the Parish and had borne a good character. On the charge being read, prisoner replied only "I did not burn the house down, I did not attempt to do so at all". He was committed to the Quarter Sessions. Bail was contested to, but as sufficient sureties were not forthcoming, the Bench endorsed the commitment so as to enable prisoner to be liberated subsequently at Exeter.

17th. October, 1887   About eight o'clock on Saturday evening, a child named Arthur Sanders, who resides with his parents at Silverton, was

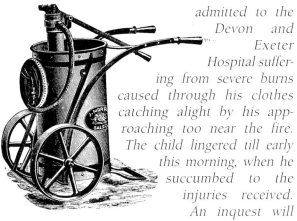

admitted to the Devon and Exeter Hospital suffering from severe burns caused through his clothes catching alight by his approaching too near the fire. The child lingered till early this morning, when he succumbed to the injuries received. An inquest will be held at the Hospital tomorrow.

11th. June, 1894 An alarming fire broke out at Silverton at about one o'clock this afternoon. Flames were first discovered in the premises occupied by Mr. Frost, butcher and farmer. They spread with alarming rapidity, and in a very short time had spread to the adjoining house of Mrs. Potter, confectioner. The Silverton Brigade of twenty-four, under Captain Short, were soon on the scene, and luckily succeeded in saving a great deal of furniture. Not-withstanding their efforts, however, the flames spread rapidly and soon four houses were ablaze, belonging to Mr. Frost, butcher, Mr. Bridgman, baker, Mrs. Sharp, and Mr. Brooks ('The Shambles'). The Exeter Brigade were communicated with by wire, and foreman Hill and firemen Down and Winsborough soon arrived with the engine and immediately got to work, but the homes, which were all thatched, were doomed, and nothing but the bare walls of five houses now remain. The Thorverton Brigade was also present. At first water was fairly plentiful being obtained from a large pond, but towards five o'clock it became rather scarce. Sergeant Major Hodges, and P.C.'s Sanders and Yeo of the Devon Constabulary were also present.

Much excitement prevailed at the time of the outbreak. Great assistance was rendered by the women of the Village. The outbreak is believed to have been due to some fat boiling over in Mr. Frost's shop. It is the largest fire which has occurred in the Village for some years. The smoke could be seen from Stoke Canon. We understand that most of the property was insured. Through the efforts of the Brigade the fire was prevented from making further headway, though fears were at one time entertained that the flames would spread to the other side of the street.

February 11, 1895 The Sunday morning quiet of Silverton was rudely broken by the cry of "Fire" raised at about half past eight. Mr. C. Biddlecombe

and members of the Fire Brigade under Mr. Short, quickly turned out with ladders and proceeded within five minutes to the scene of the outbreak, a cottage in the village owned by Mr. Stoneman of Greathill Farm, Colebrook, and occupied by Mr. F. Marley. Owing to the heat the engine could not get to work for half an hour and by that time not only had the cottage become hopelessly involved but the houses on each side had caught, and were in full blaze.

Mr. Marley lost all his furniture, and with his family had to escape by the back door, the front being a mass of flame. Mr. W. Mogridge and Miss. Padnor who lived on either side saved most of their belongings, though in a rather damaged condition. All efforts to save the cottages were unavailing and they were completely gutted having little but the bare cob walls standing. The thatched roof of a house adjoining occupied by Mr. J. Abrahams also became ignited but the fire was beaten out while water was poured on the roof of another standing on the higher side. The high wind carried the sparks for a considerable distance and some fear was expressed for the safety of houses forming the thoroughfare known as "Back Lane" but they did not receive any material damage. The fire was got under about twelve o'clock, the brigade being assisted by P.C. White and several of the neighbours. The origin of the conflagration is not definitely known but is stated that a chimney in Dr. Puddicombe's house caught fire about half an hour before the more disastrous outbreak was discovered, and it is surmised that a spark from it lodged in the thatch.

Another conjecture is that the fire was caused by the heat from a chimney of the house itself, the fact that it was first seen almost midway between the two chimneys being accounted for by the supposition that the beams of the roof had been smouldering for some days, and that the fire having then travelled about halfway across the roof, was fanned into open combustion by the gale.

The damages to the buildings is estimated at about £300 and Mr. Stoneman, the owner, is insured in the Commercial Union and West of England Office, though not, it is stated, to the full amount. None of the tenants are insured, and of them Mr. Marley especially the loss will fall heavily. Mr. Fallon will be pleased to receive subscriptions.

27th. April, 1896 About four o'clock this morning Mr. Thomas Dymond, of Fore Street, Silverton, observed flames coming from the shop of Mrs. Pridham, grocer and general dealer, and immediately raised the alarm. After calling Mr. Short, Captain of the Fire Brigade, he raised Mr. Palmer,

Silverton Parish Council.

VOLUNTARY FIRE BRIGADE RULES.

1. That this Brigade shall be called the SILVERTON PARISH COUNCIL FIRE BRIGADE VOLUNTARY.

2. That this Brigade shall be composed of 12 men as follows : 1 Captain, 1 Sub-Captain, 1 Engineer, 1 Sub-Engineer, 1 Suction Man, 7 Firemen.

3. The Brigade to attend all Fires or Practices when called upon or ordered by the Captain or next in command.

4. All members of this Brigade failing to attend two Fires or Practices in succession shall be called upon to resign, unless they give a satisfactory reason for not doing so, and in the event of a member refusing to resign the Council shall forthwith declare such member or members dismissed from the Brigade, and shall proceed to elect others to fill up any such vacancy.

5. All members of this Brigade to obey all orders of the Captain or next in command, and to take no orders from any other person or persons.

6. The Fire Engine and Brigade shall not attend any Displays or form in any Procession without first obtaining the consent of the Council.

7. The Captain to be in sole charge of all premises where a Fire takes place, and also to have sole charge of all men engaged by him. The Captain to be perfectly free to act upon his own responsibility at all Fires, and not to be appointed to any particular post or duty.

8. The Sub-Captain to be in charge of Engine when attending Fires, or in the absence of Captain to take his place.

9. The Engineer to be in charge of the Branch when attending Fires, or in the absence of the Sub-Captain to take his place.

10. The Sub-Engineer to take Engineer's place in the event of Engineer doing Sub-Captain's duty.

I, the undersigned, agree to abide by the above Rules.

Name

Dated this

Parish Council Fire Brigade rules – c.1905.

the occupant of the adjacent house. The Fire Brigade were soon on the spot, but it was seen that any attempt to save Mrs. Pridham's shop would be useless and efforts were made to ensure the safety of Mr. Palmer's. In this, however, they were unsuccessful, and both were burnt out. Mr. Palmer had previously removed a portion of his goods and furniture. Just after a young man left the house the bed in which he had been sleeping fell through the ceiling of the room below. Mrs. Pridham's loss, estimated at about £200 is insured in the Norwich Union Office, and Mr. Palmer's shop (the property of Mr. Miller) is insured for £100 in the Northern Office.

This is the fourth fire which has occurred at Silverton during the past two years. In June 1894 a row of cottages in the Square was burnt down; in the following August cottages were destroyed in Parsonage Lane; and in February 1895 a row of cottages in the Tiverton Road was burnt to the ground.

9th. July, 1934   *Shortly before 2 o'clock this afternoon a fire broke out at "Milcott", Silverton, the residence of Mr. Wilfred B. Faraday [grandson of Sir. Michael Faraday, the distinguished scientist and pioneer in the discovery of electricity and magnetism], Recorder of Barnstaple and Bideford.*

Miss. F. H. Patey, the housekeeper, who had been washing during the morning, and had needed a good fire to heat the water, was startled to hear a crackling and at the same time to see blazing thatch falling.

Miss. Patey at once sent for Mr. Faraday, and he summoned the Exeter Fire Brigade. At the same time a call had also been sent for the local Brigade which responded under Capt. E. Davis. Many willing helpers offered their services in assisting in the removal of furniture and their efforts were so successful that only a bed and a wardrobe had to be abandoned. Within half an hour of the discovery the whole roof of thatch was ablaze, the place resembling a roaring furnace. Notwithstanding the fact that the Silverton engine was an ancient one, operated by manual power – it was built in 1837 – it was used to such good purpose that the flames were prevented from spreading to other nearby property. The Exeter Brigade were handicapped in their work by a shortage of water, and had to run a hose to Lilylake, nearly half a mile distant, to obtain the necessary supply.

Nothing but the bare walls of Milcott now remain. Members of the Exeter Brigade were standing by at the time of 'phoning. The wind was in the south and flames were blown across the garden, over the farm buildings of Mr. J. Seward at the rear, but precautions promptly taken prevented the fire taking a hold there. P.S. Wilshire of Cullompton, and P.C. Pulley were quickly on the scene. The property was insured.

Mr. Ron Bowerman recalls leaving school with other lads and seeing men hauling the Silverton manual fire engine into position near the cottage in Paul's Lane, Exeter Road. The thatch roof was smouldering and people were bringing out furniture, while men on ladders were hacking away with hammers at windows and the cob walls.

Hoses were connected to a fire hydrant instead of the gutter pools, but when the signal to turn on came, the extra pressure exposed weaknesses in the pipes which sprayed all in the vicinity, particularly those manning the pump.

The Exeter Brigade had arrived, and had just taken up position behind the house, when the extra pressure caused the man holding the Silverton hose to loose his grip. Water hurled over the roof and drenched the Exeter men who returned a squirt.

The fire crew with their equipment, taken by the Girls' School on 23 September 1911.
Left to right, on the engine: Edward Davies (Fire Chief) and Walter Marsh; standing: F. Skinner,
W. Abrahams, G. Headon, A. Bright, J. Abrahams, T. Skinner, J. Stocker, W. Kenshole,
W. Carpenter, B. Adams.

The Silverton fire engine outside the Girls' School.

THE SILVERTON FIRE ENGINE

Before the village had it's own appliance, the engines from Bradninch, Thorverton and sometimes Exeter would have been called to fires in the parish. Of course all this was before the introduction of motordriven engines, so it was good old horsepower that would pull the appliance. The message to another fire station would have been sent by telegram, or a messenger would have been dispatched on horseback, a lengthy process, so it was vital that Silverton acquired its own fire engine.

Silverton, in common with many villages in the area, suffered from the destruction of house fires, due to many houses having thatched roofs. Once the thatch caught fire, it would spread very quickly from house to house, especially in windy conditions. The *Flying Post* newspaper reported on 25 May 1837 that 40 houses in the village were destroyed in one fire alone, and it is probably as a result of this disaster that Silverton purchased its own machine during that year. The Revd Tripp, who was to become the first Fire Chief, launched a fund. The Earl of Egremont, by far the largest owner of property in Silverton, together with other owners, contributed to the cost of the engine.

The year 1837 and the name 'Silverton' are painted on the appliance, but the manufacturer is unclear. There are distinguishing features from four different companies that made fire engines at that time. It appears that when an appliance was serviced a badge from the original company might have been removed and replaced by another, making it difficult to identify.

The fire engine itself did not carry any water; it was purely a pump. The suction man would have attached a hose to the rear of the engine and placed the other end in a nearby water supply, a stream or farm pond whatever was on hand. The men would pump the engine which would suck the water up the hose, and then leave via the two outlets, one on either side, connected to hoses to be directed on to the fire. A pond was built at the top of High Street at High Bullen for the purpose of holding a great deal of water (see page 38). It was quite deep, but a further reservoir was to be found in Old Butterleigh Road to replenish it should the level become low.

The village certainly had value for money from the Silverton engine, as it was used for over 100 years. In 1900, it was inspected by William Pett from the Fire Brigade Station, Exeter, who at the time described it as 'an antiquated 22-man manual'. It

Fireman Yeo in uniform.

might have been antiquated but it continued to be used in the village for another four decades until the Second World War.

One of the last fires it was used for with was that at Mr Faraday's house in Exeter Road on Tuesday 10 July 1934, when the Exeter appliance was also used. The hoses were connected to the mains supply, and not to the gutter pool for which it was designed. The extra pressure of the water sprayed out through the weaknesses in the pipes, and soaked the men manning the pump!

Photographs of the fire engine show only 12 men, led by Mr Edward Davies in full uniform. It was classed as a 22-man pump, and the other men were probably employed on a standby basis. The photograph which was taken at the Faraday fire, shows a crowd of men standing by the engine and these were probably the other ten of the crew. This fire was only a couple of hundred yards from the station situated in the Square, so there wouldn't have been the need for a horse or lorry to pull it. When a fire occurred outside the village, the men would have been called together and the horse caught, to be harnessed up to the engine before they could set off. Pumping was hard, thirsty work and men were paid 1 shilling (5 pence) for the first hour, and then 6d. (2½ pence) for each succeeding hour – they were also kept supplied with beer. The fire engine finally became redundant due to adequate cover being given by the County Fire Service. Unfortunately nowhere could be found locally to display the fire engine, and in 1950 the Parish Council handed it to the Plymouth City Museum. The station itself was rented out as a garage, as it still is today, and owned by the Parish Council.

The old fire engine was kept in fine condition, having been restored by Plymouth City firemen, and it is still in working order today. In 1976 they used it at the Civic Centre, in a sponsored attempt to break the continuous pumping record, set by a London team. Unfortunately, the men were called out so many times that day to emergencies, they had to abandon the attempt and retired after ten hours.

For many years the Silverton Engine could be seen at the Tithe Barn at Buckland Abbey, but with changes in local authority administration, a new home was sought. In 1999, after conversations with Plymouth Museum, it was agreed to transfer it to Tiverton, to be displayed alongside other items of Silverton memorabilia. The journey from Buckland was halted for a while in the Square, to enable people to see an important part of Silverton history again in familiar surroundings.

A well known photograph of Silverton Park, home of George Francis Wyndham, 4th Earl of Egremont, who died here on 2 April 1845. The building was demolished in 1901. Notice the servants standing between the pillars on the front of the building.

Stockwell House, c.1920.

Chapter 4
Principal Properties

COMBESATCHFIELD HOUSE

Records show that the Manor of Combe Sackville (originally known as Culm Reigny) was owned by a succession of families including Sir William Bonvile who exchanged it with the Courtenays of Powderham for their Manor of Southley. In 1654 it became the property of a Sidesman of Silverton, Gilbert Mortimer, who was a member of the same wealthy family that owned both Poundesland and Stockwell House.

In 1720 the property was sold to Sir Henry Langford, and on his death it was inherited by Thomas Brown, who added his benefactor's name to his own. On the death of his father,

The old Coombesatchfield, around which Silverton Park mansion was built.

Combesatchfield was left to Mr Henry Langford-Brown and his wife Dorothy. The couple had no children, and Dorothy, sister of Mrs James Coleridge of Ottery St Mary, regularly 'adopted' her nephews and nieces, after the death of her husband. In his book *The Story of A Devonshire House* Lord Coleridge refers to these holidays and describes Combesatchfield:

After the stiff fashion of the day, the two sisters always called each other 'Mrs Brown' and 'Mrs Coleridge' and at the beginning of each holiday the same formula was used: 'very well, Mrs Coleridge, I am very glad to have the boys, only remember I can't answer for them, and if they are drowned – and the ponds are very deep - or shoot themselves, or break their legs, I'm not to blame.' This protest was perhaps not unnecessary when we know that there were two of these ponds on which excursions in tubs were wont to be made, also an old pistol or two, of which the boys had full command,

and horses with which they did pretty much as they liked. Orchards too, gardens, fruit at discretion, a famous myrtle walk made Combesatchfield a paradise for the young. The mistress of the old-fashioned, stately square-built house was in keeping with its character. Too far from the Parish Church for her to walk, she always drove on Sundays in her dark green chariot with two fat horses and a postillion in drab jacket, all over buttons, with white leather breeches, top-boots, a black velvet cap surmounting all, with gold lace on the top, a very vision of splendour to youthful eyes. The postillion was always a Cookesley, a family which had hereditary claims to be part of the household. Every servant was to go to Church, and the House, solitary as it was, to be locked up. She would not relax this rule, although every year, on the Sunday before Silverton Fair, the garden, famous for its apricots, was regularly robbed during Church time.

Mrs Brown died on 11 January 1831 and the property was sold to Lord Egremont. A new house was designed around the existing structure, and the name changed to Silverton Park. When Sir John Taylor Coleridge made a nostalgic visit to the site of the unfinished mansion some years later, he recorded that:

... he entered through the portico, and after walking down a long passage came to the old green front door with its brass knocker. As he stood outside it, waiting for it to be opened, he could hardly help expecting to see old Drewe the butler, and to hear the noise of the bolt being withdrawn as in old times.

Orchard Wyndham, the Wyndham family's home near Williton, Somerset.

Blackborough House on the Blackdown Hills - another residence of the Wyndhams.
In later years it was used as a car breakers and the building is now in a very poor state.

SILVERTON PARK

Approximately one mile to the east of Silverton is the site of the mansion built for George Francis Wyndham, the fourth and last Earl Egremont. Designed in 1838 by J.T. Knowles, the house was never completed and little now remains except the stables.

The Manor of Petworth in Sussex was the seat of the Percy family, the Earls of Northumberland. When the 10th Earl died in 1670 his only heir was his daughter Elizabeth, and when 16 in 1682 her marriage was arranged to Charles Seymour, 6th. Duke of Somerset. He rebuilt Petworth and was a generous benefactor to various colleges at Cambridge University. The Duke died in 1748, and his son, the 7th. Duke, was granted the Earldoms of Nothumberland and Egremont by George ll. When he died in 1750 he also had no son, and his estates and titles were divided between his son-in-law, Sir Hugh Smithson (who changed his name to Percy) and Charles Wyndham, the son of the Duke's sister Catherine. Sir Hugh was given the Earldom of Northumberland and its estates and Charles was given Petworth, Cockermouth in Cumberland and the Earldom of Egremont.

Charles' father, Sir William Wyndham, was the descendant of an old and distinguished Norfolk family, who during the 16th century had married into a Somerset family and settled in that county at Orchard Wyndham. When Charles died in 1763 he was succeeded by his eldest son who became the 3rd Lord Egremont.

For some reason better known to themselves, this Lord Egremont did not marry the mother of his children until after the sixth was born. She used the courtesy title Mrs Wyndham but due to the succession laws of the time the Earldom did not pass to his eldest son George when he died on 11 November 1837, but to a nephew, George Wyndham, who became the 4th Earl of Egremont.

George Wyndham had been born on 6 October 1786, and on 14 November 1820 married the third daughter of the Revd William Roberts, Vice-Provost of Eton. As well as the title George Wyndham also inherited certain other property, but the family seat at Petworth in Sussex was left to his cousin, also George, who he set out to upstage

Above: *Dorothy Ayre Brown, wife of Henry Langford Brown, inhabitants of the old Coombesatchfield, whose burial vault is situated outside the west door of the church.*

Below: *Silverton Park. Only the tree on the right now remains.*

This site, a few hundred yards north of Ellerhayes, was the main entrance to Silverton Park.

Main picture: *The stone wall in Deep Cutting with a wooden doorway leading to the grounds and carriageway of Silverton Park.*
Inset: *These garden ornaments are actually two chimney pots from Silverton Park mansion.*

Main picture: *The old stables and laundry building c.1930s.*
Inset: *The same building in 2000 – little has changed.*

The underpass as it is today.

Sections of the frieze from Silverton Park.

by building a beautiful park and larger house resembling a Greek mansion.

The widow of Mr Henry Langford Brown, Dorothy Ayre Langford Brown, aunt of Samuel Taylor Coleridge of Ottery St Mary, had recently died at Combesatchfield, a house built of brick and situated in one of the most picturesque areas of Devonshire. When building Silverton Rectory, later known as Prispen House, Lord Egremont demolished the existing building. However, at Combesatchfield he created the new building by constructing it around the Brown's house, the name of which he considered not grand enough, so had it changed to Silverton Park.

Craftsmen were brought from Italy to cast the frieze that encompassed the new house and was said to portray the journey of the Israelites from Egypt to Canaan. The south front showed nine gods in relief form and Jupiter complete with eagle at the centre.

The interior was designed to include a large number of bedrooms, but they were so small that they were said to resemble cabins on a ship! Each room was equipped with a bed and a chest with two drawers built into the room, one room had no window, but was lit by a skylight that resembled an umbrella. The Earl's life at sea, during which time he had commanded the sloop H.M.S. *Hawke* in 1825, possibly explains the design of the bedrooms. However, his own bedroom was not nearly as frugal, complete as it was with an enormous yellow bath made from a solid block of marble.

In total there were 187 rooms, and supporting them beneath were 150 cellars some as low as two feet in height. There were said to be 230 marble mantelpieces, and door knobs to the principal rooms were made from amber. It was estimated that a quarter of a million pounds had been spent on the structure, a fortune in the mid-19th century.

Lord Egremont died on 2 April 1845, and although this was only eight years after inheriting the title, he had squandered so much money away that the estates never financially recovered. As well as Silverton Park and the Rectory, he had also built another mansion in the Blackdown Hills at Blackborough complete with its own church, a bridge at Kentisbeare, and he had also spent large sums on furniture and paintings. He only lived in a portion of the mansion for a few months; the remainder was left incomplete. His widow spent three months of each year at Silverton, the rest of the year being spent at Orchard Wyndham near Williton in Somerset, except for three months at Blackborough.

The original road from Ellerhayes Bridge to Silverton passed close to Silverton Park. This was not to the Earl's liking so in 1838 he obtained permission for the road to be diverted through the cutting known locally as Deep Cut to the west of the junction of the road from Bradninch. The route of the old road can still be seen on the left at a point known as 'Broad Oak', where a gate adjoins a lay-by. The drive to the stables is on the left approaching from the

Main picture: View from the Ellerhayes Bridge direction.
Left: Silverton Park sale catalogue.

village, and goes beneath the road by means of a short tunnel. It has been suggested that the earth excavated to build the cutting and tunnel was used to raise the level of the ground on the eastern side of Silverton churchyard.

On his death the Earl left many debts, and the house was put up for sale. There were negotiations to convert it into a children's home, but these fell through as agreement could not be reached to include a farm in the sale. A fortune would have been needed to complete this mansion, and it remained in an unfinished state for many years being known as 'Egremont's Folly'. The contents were sold in a sale conducted by Thompson, Rippon & Co. on 6–8 December 1892, and included amongst the antiques were two Egyptian mummies!

Hundreds of people travelled to Silverton to view the palatial house in its acres of parkland, but as no one bought it the property was sold for building material to Messrs Atkins & Taylor of Exeter, and iron girders weighing 300 tonnes and 200 tonnes of lead were stripped out and sold. Mr Herbert Fulford of Exeter auctioned portions of the house such as the mantelpieces which were sold for £50 each! One of these impressive items, made of white Italian marble, can be seen in the music room of Killerton House. The front of the house was blown up using three successive charges of dynamite, on 12 November 1901. The first charge loosened the solid pillars, the second the centre of one of the walls, and the third charge of 22 fuses was placed under two pillars which blew down half of them. The remains were left to decay for many years.

May 27 1915 saw the sale of the Silverton Estate held at the Rougemont Hotel in Exeter, when the Wyndham-owned land and properties, including many properties in Silverton as well as the majority of the farms in the locality, were auctioned. The site, stables and grounds of the mansion, together with three cottages, were included in lot 10 and reached £500 when sold to W. Ackland. The walled fruit and vegetable garden and adjoining cottage were sold to the same purchaser for £420.

In September 1926 the report of a Conservative Gymkhana held at Silverton Park remarked on 'the pathetic grandeur of decaying pillars, still erect and fragments of the frieze lying beside broken walls'.

Several artefacts from the mansion are said to be in various houses and gardens in the vicinity, including the staircase that was used at Redhayes, a large house close to Junction 29 of the M5, which sadly was totally destroyed by fire in 1993.

A view of Silverton Rectory, showing on the right the water tower, said to have been designed by Isambard Kingdom Brunel, when he was engaged on the construction of the Great Western Railway.

Prispen House in ruins after the fire of July 1990. (J. Tree)

PRISPEN HOUSE

Prispen House, formerly the Silverton Rectory, was built on the site of a building that was possibly as old as St Mary's Church. Richard Bryan, Silverton's rector from 1656 to 1659, wrote in the terrier* signed by him that the Parsonage contained 33 rooms, a paved hall, and cellars, four of which were paved and the remainder earthen. There were 13 outhouses, a couple of barns and three stables, also 2½ acres of gardens and ponds covering a further half-acre.

No record has been found detailing the condition of this building, but in 1839 this ancient property was demolished by order of Lord Egremont. A new Rectory was built, from a design by Richard Carver, for the new incumbent the Revd Dr Charles Tripp, son of Lord Egremont's favourite lawyer.

The new house contained 18 rooms, 13 offices and storerooms, plus three lavatories. The stables included stalls for four horses, a harness room, coach house and a carthorse stable. Later a dining room and drawing room with four bedrooms above were added at the northern end, and a tower to the south. The rooms were low and those of the extension high, so the ceilings of the old bedrooms were raised by about six feet in order to give them a uniform height.

When the Revd Fox-Strangways became the rector in 1866, his wife had two enormous windows cut in the wall of rooms that were then used for the children's nurseries. It is recorded that some thought that these enlarged windows spoilt the design.

Springs in the hill supplied the house with water. A double pond in the hollow ground below Prispen, previously mentioned in the 17th-century document, and said to date from the 13th century, provided fish for the household on Fridays and for the 40 days of Lent.

In 1937 the Rectory and a substantial amount of the remaining Glebe Land were sold. A retired Army officer, Major Stuart Nicholson, purchased Prispen, and during the Second World War he trained the local Home Guard at the house. On 6 September 1952 the Major died, but his widow, Mrs Dorothy Nicholson, lived at Prispen House until her 100th year in 1987 (although she died later the same year).

The house and surrounding land were purchased by a development company, and although listed as a building of special historical and architectural interest, the District Council granted permission for it to be converted into flats. During the early hours of Monday 20 July 1990 a disastrous fire mysteriously broke out causing damage so severe that what remained of the house was demolished. Various plans have been drawn up for the use of the site, including the most recent in June, 2000, for the construction of nine houses and six flats on this historical location.

* A terrier is a legal document describing the site, boundaries, acreage, etc. of lands privately owned by persons or corporations.

Above: *A 1930s view of the Rectory later named 'Prispen House'.*
Above right: *Prispen House from the Mead.*

Dunsmore – tradition has it that this was the refuge of King Charles I's baby daughter Henrietta during the Civil War

Panelled bedroom at Dunsmore showing ornate ceiling.

DUNSMORE

Situated almost a mile south of the village centre, Dunsmore is one of the most interesting properties in the area. It was one of the farms of the Royal Manor of Silverton although the name was not mentioned in the Domesday Book.

During the 14th century Dunsmore was separated from the Manor, and became the property of Phillip de Dunsmore. In 1333 his daughter and heiress, Theophila Phillipa, married Robertus de Fursdon, son of Walter Fursdon of Fursdon near Thorverton.

In 1623 John Were, Counsellor at Law and prominent Royalist, owned Dunsmore. During September 1643 Exeter became the headquarters of King Charles' forces in the West Country, and Queen Henrietta Maria was staying in the city at Bedford House, home of the Earls of Bedford. Here on 16 June 1644 she gave birth to Princess Henrietta Anne. Exeter came under siege, and on 4 April 1646 surrendered to Cromwell's army. Princess Henrietta was allowed to leave with her staff, and strong local tradition has it that she was first taken to Dunsmore. A beautifully panelled oak room there

Above: *Sundial at Dunsmore.* Below: *A modern photograph of Dunsmore showing the ancient wall and archway.*

has since been known as 'Princess Henrietta's room'.

During the next 100 years various descendants of John Were inherited Dunsmore, but in 1782 it was sold to a John White, and for the next century changed hands many times. By 1882 it was owned by the Rt Hon. William Henry Smith, Cabinet Minister, First Lord of the Admiralty, and the founder of W.H. Smith the booksellers. William (Lord Hambleden) wanted his farms to be models, and took a keen interest in the buildings and the operations. The pitch of the tithe barn was lowered, the thatch replaced by slate, and other fine farm buildings erected in the style of his other properties in the locality: Pownsland, Hayne, Rewe Barton and Heazille.

In 1911 Charles Bere purchased the farm from Lord Hambleden for £7000, and resided here until 1921, when he retired to Cockhayne in Exeter Road, Silverton. Dunsmore was next owned by Edward Wedemyer, a director of Plymouth Breweries, who was a bachelor and said to be more interested in having a good life than running a farm. He lost money and had to sell Dunsmore when Mr William Ackland acquired it. The farm is still owned by his descendants today.

Silverton Mill as it looked in 1916.

Cutting paper at Silverton Paper Mill.

Chapter 5
The Silverton Paper Mill

On Tuesday 29 June 1999 the speculation of weeks gone by was confirmed by the news that Silverton Paper Mill was to close at the end of September. Owned by the St Regis Paper Company, the number of men employed had decreased since earlier in the century when, after agriculture, it had been Silverton's main source of employment. Its closure spelt a sad chapter in the story of an industry that had given employment to generations of Silverton families, and the Devon Valley Mill at Hele has now become the only working mill in the immediate vicinity.

Situated on the banks of the River Culm just in the parish of Broadclyst, the Silverton Paper Mill had been of great importance to the economy of the village for more than two centuries. It was one of many mills that had developed beside local rivers in order to utilise the water for power and processing. In 1791 there were five recorded within two miles of Bradninch, plus others at Rewe, Thorverton, Upper and Lower Huxham, Up Exe and at Stoke Cannon.

The earliest known record relating to the site is the mention of a lease dated in the 16th year of the reign of Henry VIII (1524/25) when it was held by a Rauffe Bennet. Two centuries later a letter describes a tucking or fulling mill producing woollen cloth. An indenture dated 6 February 1766 assigned to Richard Morgan, millwright of Bradninch by Saint Barb. Sydenham of Priory, and Sir Thomas Dyke Acland of Killerton, which describes the plot of ground containing a set of water grist mills which had burnt down and were in ruins and known as Etherly's Mills. This land also contained a garden and an island totalling two acres situated in Broadclyst Parish and previously in the tenure of John Knight. Contained in the lease was the condition that Richard Morgan, aged 31, his wife Mary of the same age, and their daughter Sarah aged seven, were to rebuild the mill at their own cost within two years, with the head weir, mill ponds and the dwelling-house, and also construct a further mill for the dressing of leather.

The mill changed hands and was further developed, and in 1783 a paper mill was also built by William Matthews, who had been responsible for the papermaking at Hele Mill, changing it from the production of flour. William was succeeded on his death in 1790 by John Matthews, and a lease drawn up in 1811 between him and Sir Thomas Dyke Acland, included the land that contained the water grist mill and the dwelling house erected since a fire that had occurred during John Matthews' ownership. John also built Bridge House and in 1828 leased the 'Mill Meadow' that had been occupied until his death by John Veitch, a young Scottish gardener, who had been brought to Devon by Sir Thomas Acland to 'lay out the Park at Killerton'.

After the death of John Matthews in 1841 the property was assigned to Charles Matthews and Richard Martin for the purpose of papermaking, and in 1864 a siding was constructed to enable the mill use of rail freight on the main Bristol to Exeter railway line. The year 1873 saw the mill again sold for what was to be the first of three times in the next 20 years. A period of stability was to commence in 1892 with the sale of Bridge Mills to Reed & Smith, a name with which it would be associated for the next 86 years. During this period many alterations were made to the site commencing with the adaptation of a building for use as a Methodist chapel in the late-19th century. A new office block was constructed at the time of Queen Victoria's Jubilee in 1897, and the building of workers' houses at Ellerhayes began in 1900.

Bridge Mill was unique in England as it produced paper from esparto grass which was imported by sea in bales from North Africa, where it grew, to the port of Watchet in West Somerset. From here the bales were transported by rail to the mill's sidings, and stored in the large building with over gantry on the north side of the site. The grass was then passed through a rotating duster which extracted the dust, a substance that was similar to powdered wax, and was collected in very finely woven bags and sold to be used in the manufacture of shoe polish.

The grass was then fed into one of four large digesters, which processed it under steam pressure in a solution of caustic soda for about six hours to remove the lignin (the cement-like substance that

Top left: *The River Culm in flood at the mill c.1970.*

Above: *Arthur Jefferson wrapping reams of paper at Silverton Mill.*

Left: *Mrs Edith Diamond sorting paper at Silverton Mill in the 1970's.*

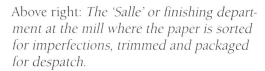

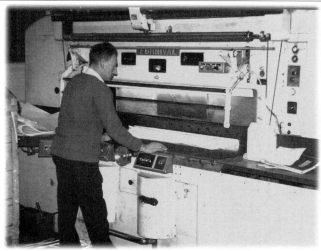

Above right: *The 'Salle' or finishing department at the mill where the paper is sorted for imperfections, trimmed and packaged for despatch.*

Above: *Guillotine being operated by E. Chowings and D. 'Jack' Tree.*

Right: *Trimming large sheets of paper on a guillotine at Silverton Mill.*

(All photographs this page, J. Tree)

binds the plant fibres together). The caustic soda was reclaimed by burning the liquid from the boilers in a device called a 'roaster', which converted it back to powder to be re-used. Various other processes were required before the pulp was ready for bleaching and finally processing through a 'presse pate', a machine which drained and sucked away the water, the resulting pulp then being used to make paper.

Esparto fibres are short which gives paper a high opacity much in demand for book papers, and they are usually used together with imported wood pulp. When the supply of esparto grass was halted during the Second World War, straw from local farms was used, and a baler was transported around the area to collect it. With the large shed not being used for the storage of the North African grass, the Admiralty used it instead for the storage of torpedoes that were assembled in the mill buildings at Stoke Canon, and these were regularly seen being carried on lorries through the Square.

During 1939 Reed & Smith obtained a contract from the Admiralty for the production of purified cellulose paper to be converted to nitrocellulose (gunpowder). The terms of the contract required that an Admiralty chemist and three shift assistants were employed, a feature that continued for the duration of the war. During this time the Head Chemist at Silverton Mill, Mr Bill Traill, was required to analyse the fibre type and dyes used in a German War Ration Card to obtain the grey-blue colour. As well as two types of wood fibre he discovered that it contained red cow hair to make it difficult to counterfeit! It also contained a watermark of the German Eagle, and when similar paper was produced a Dandy Roll to incorporate the watermark was supplied by the Security Services. In addition to these cards the mill also assisted in the war effort by making the paper backing that was covered with a film of aluminium and dropped by planes to disrupt RADAR.

The paper-making industry, like most manufacturing businesses, was to see great changes after the end of the Second World War. Electricity and computerisation superceded large sections of the workforce. In 1891 about 70 men were employed, and this was to increase to a peak in the early 1960s to some 350 staff, before the reduction over the next 40 years. The papermaker's skills, which were often handed down from father to son, were required to adapt to this new technology to enable the mill to remain competitive in the new world-wide market. Unlike previous centuries when the competition was the mill further downstream, the competition now was in Europe, America or Japan.

In 1978 Reed & Smith sold Silverton Mill to the St Regis Corporation of America. It returned to British ownership once more in 1985 with the formation of the St Regis Paper Company (UK) Ltd but this was to prove to be the final owner after four centuries as a working mill. The future use of the area has still to be decided. The land on which the buildings stand has been owned by the National Trust since Killerton and the remainder of the Acland Estates were given to them in 1944 by Sir Richard Acland.

A new paper-making machine assembled in the engineering workshop prior to being assembled in the machine house. MD, Mr William Tweedie, and Sir Arthur Reed, in foreground, 1952.

A view of the north face of the church, with two large trees in the churchyard at the time.

The interior of the church, c.1900, still lit by oil lamps.

Chapter 6
Parish Church and Chapels

SILVERTON PARISH CHURCH

The present church dates from about 1450, though much altered since, and almost certainly has always been dedicated to St Mary the Virgin. There must have been an earlier building on the site, as the list of rectors goes back to 1273. It was possibly situated to the west of the present church more or less where the old mortuary stands (now sadly in a ruined state), that being the highest point of the churchyard. It is even possible that there could have been a church or chapel and grave-yard here from Saxon times, which would then have been the centre of the village. The remains of a chapel supposedly dedicated to St Mary are shown to the east of the church on early Ordnance Survey maps, although nothing is now visible above ground. Such an attribution is dubious, however, as no record can be found of such a chapel in the parish and, since these remains were outside the curtilage of the churchyard, they are more likely to have been the foundations of a large domestic building, which could very easily have been in the vicinity of the church.

The church is largely built of local volcanic trap stone, probably taken from any one of a number of quarries that existed in the area. It is built in the perpendicular style of architecture with large four-light windows to the aisles. At the west end is a low, but impressive, two-stage tower with two diagonal buttresses on the western corners, a buttress where the tower abuts the porch, and a stair turret at the north-east corner.

The porch on the south side of the church contains an image niche over the outer arch and the remains of a stoup by the inner doorway, the basin itself having apparently been removed. There is a fine old oak door, the base-plate of the door handle bearing the date 1713 and the initials 'TW' and 'W'

West door and tower.

(churchwardens?). This may have been the date of a repair rather than its original construction, and the door was probably once the inner door to the church. A 'scratch dial' is inserted into the wall of the stair turret on the south side about one and a half metres above the ground.

The yew tree standing in the churchyard near the south door, some 27 feet in circumference, is estimated to be around 1000 years old! Also by the path leading to the porch is the base of the 'Palm Cross', doubtless destroyed by the icono-clasts in the mid-16th century. This cross would have featured in the Palm Sunday ceremonials, and it seems also as an important stopping point on the annual Rogationtide processions or 'pilgrimages' which took place through the parish from Babylon to Criss Cross (Christ's Cross) and elsewhere to bless the fields and the crops.

The church has eight bells. Silverton had rejoiced in a peal of four bells as early as 1553. These bells were replaced in 1743 by five bells, which were cast by William Evans of Chepstow. A sixth bell was added in 1845, cast locally by Pannel & Son, of Cullompton, and which was recast by Gillett & Johnson in 1914. In the 1930s it became apparent that the old wooden frame had become decayed and the brass bearings worn, with the result that cracks were beginning to appear in the structure of the tower. So in 1937 a new iron and steel frame was mounted ten feet below the old frame. The whole peal was re-tuned by John Taylor of Loughborough and at the same time the opportunity was taken to add two more bells.

The sequence of building which has produced the light and airy church interior enjoyed today is not easy to deduce. It is likely that the 15th-century church was without aisles until a north aisle was built by the bequest of John Swyfmore, who died in 1478. He left £40 'for the edificacion and billing of a newe ambelatory in the north syde of the said churche' in

Two pictures left: *The porch door and the door handle clearly showing the date 1713.*

Below: *The alms chest.*

Left centre: *Screen of St Anne's Chapel in memory of Jane, Countess of Egremont, who died 18 December 1876.*

Bottom:
The 'Hudd', a wooden shelter that was carried to the graveside during wet funerals and used to keep the rector's wig dry.

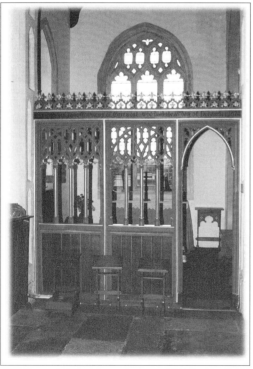

Right: *The scratch dial, a crude sundial scratched in stone with an iron nail driven into the centre to cast a shadow.*

❁ Church Roof ❁

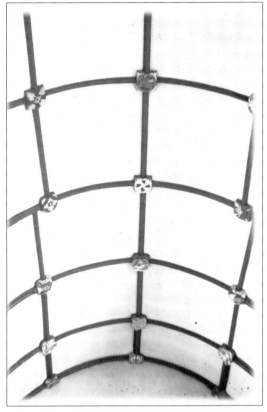

Top: *Medieval wagon roof. During 1957, John (Jack) Perrin reconstructed some of the 36 bosses and also added some new designs.*

Clockwise from left: *Ox – St Luke; Blessed Virgin Mary; Tudor rose; Eagle – St John; the pair of hands are a carving by Mr Perrin; Bishop Bourne.*

order to create a chantry, and endowed a priest 'to synge in the said North Ile'. Sir Nicholas Wadham and the then incumbent, Lawrence Dobell, who was rector from 1519 to 1549, founded a further chantry, 'the fraternytye of our ladye at Sylverton'.

Prosperity due to the revival of the cloth industry and trade began to return to Devon in the early years of the 16th century, and a great phase of church building took place throughout the county. The old church must have appeared mean and not nearly impressive enough for the borough of Silverton which doubtless successive manorial lords hoped one day might grow into a thriving market town. A major reconstruction of the interior of the church appears to have been undertaken by Dobell, and the pillars and aisles (and possibly also the roof) may have come from this period. The pillars are constructed of Beer stone, and are ornamented with fine carved capitals. Three have image niches. Lawrence Dobell himself is commemorated in the capital on the easternmost pillar of the northern aisle by the carving of a rebus comprising two grid-irons, the symbol of St Lawrence, and his name 'do bell' inscribed on the scroll facing into the church.

The rood screen was probably erected at about this time, and originally went across the full width of the church between the pillars one bay up from the east end of the present nave. This would have separated the nave from the chancel, so that the nave would then have been one bay shorter than at present. The chancel, with its side-altars in the aisles, occupied the space to the east of the screen and continued beyond the chancel arch to only about half the length of the present chancel, stopping short of the end of the vestry. The small door in the south aisle once lead to the staircase turret which gave access to the rood loft on the top of the screen for the various ceremonies which would have been performed there, and though now plastered over, the shape of the upper door can still be seen in the wall. But this screen was to have only a short life in its entirety, for at the Reformation, the rood itself would have been torn down by order of the reformers. The remains of the base of the screen appear to have survived into the 19th century, when the square posts of the frame are described as having been topped with large green and gold carved pineapples. This was finally removed on the very substantial rebuilding of the church which took place in 1862-3. Only a fragment of the original screen now remains in two bays of the 19th-century screen that encloses the St Anne's Chapel.

The gallery at the west end of the church would appear, from the design of its supporting pillars, to have been erected some time around the mid-17th century, a time when many Devon churches were building such galleries to cope with the growing

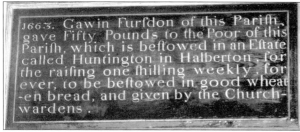

Top: *Distributing the free bread in the 1940s.*
Left to right: Mrs Lucy Coombes, Mrs Yeo, Freddy
Down, Mrs Gooding, Mary Gill, Pam Pearce,
Revd Shelmerdine, Verger Mr Sidney Ellis.
Above: *Charity plaque of Gawin Fursdon.*

population. In 1734, however, the gallery was moved forward to give greater space, and the ten front panels record the numerous charitable benefactions to the parish. Access to this gallery was by an outside stair through a door in what is now the window at the west end of the south aisle. A smaller gallery was constructed above the main gallery in 1763 to house the choir and the band, which at one time comprised a base viol, two clarinets, and a flute.

The inhabitants of the hamlet of Up Exe, the ancient chapel there having been closed, also attended Silverton Parish Church. A gallery was built in the south aisle to accommodate these parishioners, possibly about the same time as the west-end gallery was extended. Access to the 'Up Exe gallery' was by means of the former rood-screen staircase. The effect of this gallery, however, was to cut out a great deal of light from the church, and to remedy this skylights were inserted in the roof of the nave, the boarded-up remains of which are still in evidence.

By the mid-19th century there was clearly very considerable pressure on space to seat the growing number of parishioners, and going on contemporary descriptions of the interior, the church must also have looked very cluttered, dark and old-fashioned. Recommendations for a very substantial rebuilding were made by the Exeter Diocesan Architectural Society at the request of the rector, Dr Tripp, in 1842. This included a grandiose scheme to build a transept on the north side to accommodate the Egremont family pew, but Lord Egremont died before this could be undertaken.

It was not until 1860 that the proposal was revisited, and by this date the chancel had fallen into a very dilapidated state. Apart from the transept, the rest of the plans for the restoration of the church were carried out more or less as originally conceived. Work started in 1862 and was completed the following year. The architect was John Hayward with Edward Ashworth as consultant.

The nave of the church was extended eastwards by the removal of the remains of the rood screen, and the chancel beyond the arch was more or less doubled in length. The Up Exe gallery was removed, and the present pulpit introduced, although then against the south side of the chancel arch. New pine pews, of which most still remain in place, provided seating for nearly 500. The churchyard was enlarged along its eastern boundary by the addition of a strip of ground given to the church by Lord Ilchester and the trustees of Lord Egremont. The church was re-consecrated by Bishop Trower of Gibraltar on 27 June 1863.

The chapel to the north of the chancel was built on to the church in 1880. It is said that this was designed as an organ chamber to accommodate the new organ, but the quality of the carved ceiling would suggest that perhaps this was originally conceived as a chapel and was only later adopted for this purpose. A screen was inserted in the arch created between the aisle and the organ chamber, inscribed as being in memory of 'Jane, Countess of Egremont, who died 18 December 1870', which incorporates a small part of the original rood screen.

The organ, originally built by Messrs J.W. Walker and Sons in 1880, was rebuilt and moved to the west-end gallery in 1972. A new chapel was created out of the space vacated by the organ, which was dedicated to St Anne on 26 July 1973.

The windows to the aisles are large, each with four lights. Those in the north aisle contain clear glass, and the views over the surrounding hills give the church a very special quality appropriate to a rural parish. The stained glass in the south aisle is by Warrington, signed and dated 1859, and that in the east-end window inserted during the refurbishment of 1880 is by Ward and Hughes.

Above: *The eight church bells on the church path before being hung in time to ring out for the Coronation of King George VI in 1937.*

Right: *A photograph of the belfry showing the bells and mechanism.*

The wagon roof of the nave is plastered and ribbed, with fine carved bosses at the intersection of the ribs. The roof was restored in 1957, and these bosses are the work of Jack Perrin who reconstructed a number of the original bosses and carved new ones to fill the blank spaces. One of the bosses on the south side of the roof is the head of Bishop Gilbert Bourne, the original of which is on display in the church. Bishop Bourne had been the chaplain to Queen Mary, but on the accession of Elizabeth had refused to take part in the consecration of Archbishop Parker and to subscribe to the Oath of Supremacy, as a result of which he was removed from his see of Bath and Wells and placed in the 'gentle custody' of Dr George Carew, the then rector of Silverton and Dean of Windsor. Bishop Bourne spent the rest of his life in Silverton. He died on 10 September 1569, and is buried in the church. It has been suggested that this boss, which would originally have been in the former chancel, may have been set in the roof over his burial place.

At the back of the church is an iron-clamped alms chest, as required for all churches by the Ecclesiastical Canons of 1603, with its three locks; the rector and churchwardens each had a key to one, so that the chest could not be opened unless all three were present. Also kept in the church is the 'hudd', a wooden portable shelter, looking rather like a sentry box, in which the priest could stand at the graveside in inclement weather to conduct the interment.

There is, therefore, much of interest to see in Silverton church, and a great deal of history associated with it. But perhaps of most importance, here is a much-loved and cared-for church that has been the focus of a worshipping community for countless generations of Silverton inhabitants.

Above: *View of the church showing the ancient yew tree and the base of the Palm Cross.*

Right: *Stone carved image of St Mary over the arch of the south porch.*

METHODISM

In 1834 John Norman, a basket maker from Parsonage Lane, and his landlord John Perriman, obtained a licence to preach in their house. A chapel was later built here at a cost of £400, and it was used to hold services from 1846. The building was later occupied as a dwelling house for many years until it was demolished in 1964, and the site used to build what are now numbers 7 and 9 Parsonage Lane. The current Methodist church is situated in Fore Street, on the corner of Parsonage Lane, and was officially opened on 9 December 1914. The site was given by Mr W. H. Reed, a Director of the Paper Mill, and cost £830. Mr Reed also contributed 10 per cent of the building costs.

John Wesley (1703-91), who is seen to be the founder of Methodism, was an Anglican rector and remained so throughout his lifetime. It was after his death that a separate denomination was formed. Mr Wesley visited the West Country on many occasions, and it is highly likely that he passed through Silverton. His diary reveals that in November 1739 he journeyed on horseback from Exeter to Blundells School in Tiverton to pay his respects to his recently widowed sister-in-law, whose late husband Samuel Wesley had been headmaster of the school.

Over the years the Methodist church has sought to play an active role in the community and the wider world. During the Second World War when evacuees were accommodated in the village, and when American servicemen were billeted in the area, the church was full to overflowing, and there have been similar times since. One example was when the late Lord Tonypandy, the former Speaker of the House of Commons, was invited to preach by Sir Robin Maxwell-Hyslop, the then MP for Tiverton.

The Christian witness of its people has continued over the last 90 plus years, and many have found a spiritual home within its fellowship. Currently worship is celebrated each Sunday morning and evening. There are monthly meetings for both Prayer and Bible Study, and a programme for children and young people on Fridays and Sundays. The church is pleased to provide a meeting place for the Day Centre for the less mobile, and for various village groups that use the warm and comfortable accommodation.

Above: *The present Methodist church in Fore Street.*
Top left: *Old Methodist chapel in Parsonage Lane. This was converted to a dwelling after the new building was opened in 1914. This photograph shows Mrs Amy Carpenter in the doorway. The railings just visible in the left foreground were some of the few that remained after the Second World War, and were transferred to the house next to the Old Church Gallery. They probably survived the war effort because the lane was too narrow for the scrap lorry to negotiate!*

The chapel choir in the 1930s. Left to right, back row: Dolly Bryant, Ruby Strickland, Minnie Nicholls, ?, Mrs Dymond, Mrs Hutchings, Mrs Chudley, Wally Sussex; middle: Mr Wallond, Mr and Mrs Fred Bryant, Jack Gooding, Jack Rosser, Maurice Bryant; front: Jean Bryant, Winnie Vittles, Patsy Batten, Cynthia Brady, ?, Dennis Strickland, Fred Gooding.

Chapel choir in the 1950s. Left to right, back row: Ernest Bryant, Louisa Petherick, Daisy Bryant, Frederick Bryant, Revd Douglas Wollen, Harry Warren, Elizabeth Chudley, Reginald Wolland, Patricia Gilpin, Eileen Brook, William Chudley, Frederick Petherick; seated: Dolly Bryant, Hetty Hutchings, Nancy Webb, Nancy Lamacraft, Shirley Brook, Hazel Bryant, Michael Vinnicombe, Mervyn Lamacraft, Helen Piney, Susan Vinnicombe, Jill Sinclair, Mavis Hutchings, Ann Parsons.

SILVERTON EVANGELICAL CHURCH

Before the Second World War a small congregation drawn from Silverton and the surrounding areas met in an old pound barn at Burn Farm for Sunday services and an afternoon Sunday School. The old organ and pulpit still exist within this building.

After the outbreak of war the congregation was joined by an orphanage of 21 French children looked after by Ken and Pricilla Johnson. They had all fled from France ahead of the invading German forces and had come to live at Livinghayes House. Mr Don Brady remembers Ken driving a jeep, and with his finely chiselled features and full beard recalls local children calling him 'Jesus in the Jeep'.

The children and the Johnsons used to walk to Burn each morning and evening for the services. During Sunday afternoons a service, held at Livinghayes, was attended by many Silvertonians some of whom are still around to remember the wonderful times they had there. The seeds of the present church developed from these meetings until in May 1944 a purpose-built, lined wooden hut was brought from Langport in Somerset and erected on land close to the present entrance to Hederman Close.

In 1955 a two-roomed Gospel hall was erected on land donated by a member of the congregation, Mr Henry Alford. The congregation met the cost of the building which could seat 80 people, with space when the second room was opened up for a further 20-30. During the 1980s the congregation felt that the building was not big enough to meet the demands of day and evening activities, especially the growing congregation that was likely to come as the village expanded. A new extension was designed to have multi-purpose use and a capacity to seat 250 at special events.

In 1989 a 'wrap round' extension was added to the existing building to provide the church that can be seen today. Again the congregation met the costs

and all assisted in the building work under the guidance of the main builder Mr David German an Elder of the Church.

SEC, as the church is known locally, is active in the life of the village and has a regular congregation of between 60 and 75 each week. The village playgroup has used the facilities since 1990. The church draws people from a ten-mile radius, and has regular contact with churches and Christian organisations all over the world. It is an Independent Free Church, which is administered by a group of appointed Elders and Deacons, and is a member of a national body – The Evangelical Alliance.

Top: *Interior view of the Chapel showing the pulpit and organ (harmonium) still in situ.*

Above: *Burn Farm with the old chapel in the foreground, and the Burn River flowing by.*

Left: *Evangelical church in School Road.* (All J.Tree)

THE BOOK OF SILVERTON

Up Exe Chapel

The old chapel at Up Exe, for some years now a dwelling, can be seen across the fields almost hidden by trees as one goes to take the Exeter road. It has quite an interesting history and many connections with Silverton.

These small chapels dotted about the country were probably served by the clergy of some of the lesser monasteries, before the Dissolution. The architecture is of 13th-century style, and there is a good door and remains of three single-lancet windows on the south side and a small lancet west window. There is also a three-light east window of very plain early decorated style, but this fell out when restoration was commenced. The chapel had been used as dwellings for several generations.

The Revd P. Williams of Rewe thought to restore it for services under licence from the Bishop and obtained the building by an exchange with a Mr C.A.W. Troyte. With new cottages having been built and the railway running through, the inhabitants were eager to have a church of their own. Mr R. Medley Fulford was the architect and Mr Short of Silverton was contracted for the alterations which were estimated to cost £269.6s.9d. Sir Thomas D. Acland supplied stone from Killerton and donations were received from Church Societies and others promised by various people. Thus the chapel was ready for use in 1889. There had been a gallery for

Main picture: *Gospel Mission van which toured the area in the early 1900s.*

Above: *Up Exe Chapel.*

Up Exe in the south aisle of Silverton Church, and the plastered over doorway to it can be seen.

In later years the services came into the ministry of the rector at Silverton and one member of the congregation recalls going down to play the harmonium for the hymns. When the chapel ceased to be needed for worship it was sold in the 1970s for conversion. The understanding was that the last parish to hold services there should benefit by the sale so Silverton Church was able with the proceeds to buy the Old School for use as a hall. This was later sold, enabling the church to build the present office in the churchyard.

88

Chapter 7
Education

The first mention of education in Silverton appears in an application by the rector, the Revd Richard Bryant, dated 1686 to the Bishop of Exeter, requesting a licence to enable the curate, Mr Aaron Locke, to teach at the Village School. This was due to the death of the headmaster Mr John Hopkins. The site of this school is not known and neither is its source of income, but there is in existence a testimonial written c.1700, sent by the rector, Richard Troyte, and other parishioners, to the Bishop of Exeter. This document nominated Joseph Dunscombe for a licence to teach and instruct children in 'the faculty of reading the English tongue and in the art of writing and cyphering.' Dunscombe was described as 'a person of very sober conversation, who duly frequents his church.'

John Richards, a London Merchant who had been born in Silverton, died in 1729 and left in his will what was in those days the considerable sum of £1200, to build and endow a boys' school in the village. Nine trustees were appointed and a plot of land that had

Above: *Mrs Lily England, a teacher for the Girls' School, c.1905.*
Below: *The Girls' School c.1905.*

been the site of three cottages destroyed by fire was purchased from George Fursdon for the sum of 12 guineas. This plot was 'between the Exeter/Tiverton road and the 'shambles', and bordering on the south side the lands of Frances Were, Esq.' Two farms at Cheriton Fitzpaine, named Stockton and Grew, were also purchased for £1120 as an endowment, which was expected to have a yearly value of £55p.a. The trustees gave themselves authority to elect the schoolmaster to teach the boys to read, and to write:

... without any fees or reward. But if the said Schoolmaster do neglect the School or do anything unworthy of that trust, he shall be liable to be turned out.

It was intended to contract workmen or a 'Master Builder' to complete the school-house by 25 March 1733, within the remaining budget of £203.6s.0d., but the trustees substantially underestimated the cost of building. After paying for the mason, Christopher Lock (his bill

Silverton Girls' School weaving class, 1936.
Left to right, back row: Bertha Stradling, Joan Scott, Margaret Ball, Nellie Manning,
Betty Selley;
front: Gladys Dymond, ?, June Hutchings, Adelade Hutchings, Doreen Bowles, Marion Freethy,
Eileen Chidgey, Jean Saunders.

Woodwork class taken by Charles Yeo, schoolmaster, c.1935.

amounting to £144.17s.5d.), and for the various materials there was a deficiency of £200, a sum that was borrowed from Mr Richards, Mr Land and Mr Russell. The building was continually referred to as the 'schoolhouse' due to it also being the home of the headmaster. This continued until the early 1900s, with the headmaster living in the part of the building that now adjoins the butcher's shop. A stone was placed on the outside of the building, in commemoration of the legacy from John Richards. This reads:

This Charity School was erected and Endowed by the gift of £1200 by John Richards of London, Merchant a Native of this Parish by his will dated the 14 day of November, 1724 proved in Doctors Commons by John Richards of London Esq. His Nephew and Executor.

In 1751 the trustees were:

Robert Comings of Silverton, Yeoman
Thomas Carpenter senior of Silverton, Yeoman
John Richards of Islington, Middlesex, Esq.
William Land of Hayne in Silverton, Esq.
Peter Beavis of Clist House, Devon, Esq.
John Richards of Silverton
Thomas Carpenter, junior of Silverton
John Channon of Silverton
Robert Channon of Silverton
Nathaniel Warren of Silverton

Over the years many notable names have been listed amongst the trustees, including: Sir Thomas Dyke Acland (7th. Bt.) of Killerton, George Fursdon of Fursdon, Henry Langford Brown of Combesatchfield, James Buller of Downes, Crediton, The Hon. and Right Revd George Pelham, Lord Bishop of Exeter, Right Hon. George Wyndham, Earl of Egremont of Silverton Park, Sir Thomas Dyke Acland (9th.Bt.), James Wentworth Buller, Sir Thomas Dyke Acland (10th. Bt.). The following were schoolmasters:

Mr Henry Blighe   1733
Mr Thomas Carpenter *
Mr Joseph Head   1775
Mr James Passmore   1794
Mr Samuel Hopkins   1850
Mr John Mills Higgins   1874
Mr John Alexander Fallon 1879 **
Mr Tipper   1919

* Mr Thomas Carpenter was son of the churchwarden of that name, who was also Treasurer of the School Trust.
** Mr Fallon was the last Mayor of Silverton, and said to be a strict disciplinarian, who combined his school

duties with that of church organist, choirmaster, a leading member of the Town Band, and a founder member of the Silverton Men's Club.

Mr Blighe's and Mr Carpenter's salary was £25 per annum. Mr Passmore received 6 guineas per quarter, until in 1849 the trustees agreed that the headmaster's salary should not be less than £70, and that £10 was also to be given to provide books, slates and stationery for the children.

The trustees had the power to 'turn out a schoolmaster who neglected his duties'. This power was used in 1794 when the parishioners raised a petition against the then headmaster, Mr Joseph Head, in which it was alleged that he:

... almost totally neglects the school, and is not himself in the same one fourth part of the school hours, and pays very little or no attention to the children that are placed under him, and keeps them on one lesson sum or copy for several weeks together, and that the children when they leave the school are nearly as ignorant as when first placed under his care so that the inhabitants [are] forced to send their children to school at a considerable distance and at great trouble and expense.

In the year 1794, 15 January saw a meeting of the trustees at which these charges were considered, and several parishioners were called to give evidence against Mr Head. It was stated that the headmaster

Right: *Plaque over entrance to the Girls' and Infants' School at the junction of Coach, School and Park Roads.* Below: *Plaque on the outside wall of Richards Endowed School.*

was often 'in liquor' and that he was 'leading an immoral life' but no record exists of Mr Head's defence, except that only one person was not in favour of his removal.

On 13 February 1794 the trustees appointed Mr James Passmore of Bridport as the headmaster of the Free School of Silverton. Mr Head was awarded the sum of 6 guineas a year for the rest of his life, in consideration of his expenditure in repairing and altering the schoolhouse, to be paid from profit and rent of the Trust's estate. In the Report of the School in 1830 it was stated:

The present Headmaster was appointed in 1794... he receives the rent from the Estates at Cheriton Fitzpaine, and in respect thereof instructs all the boys of the Parish, not only the sons of the poor, but also of the farmers and others whose parents think proper to send them to school, in reading writing and arithmetic, partly on the Madras System. No particular age is fixed for the time of the boys coming to, or their removal from, school. A woman is paid by the master as an assistant to teach the younger boys. The average number of scholars is about seventy. Books are at present provided for this school from the private charity of the Rector.

At this time the headmaster, 'as the person most interested', let the farms at £130 per annum, less deductions for rates, taxes and repairs, which left about £90 per annum.

Although the income from the farms varied from year to year, it was always sufficient to pay the headmaster's salary, and the maintenance of the school building along with that of the farms themselves. However, Mr Passmore, in consideration of the substantial increase in salary that he received in 1849, was expected to finance the repairs to the schoolhouse himself. Towards the end of his 56 years in office, he was considered by the trustees to be neglecting this arrangement. His son, James junr, anxious that no official action should be taken against his father that would cause him distress, proposed in a letter in 1846 that he would pay the sum of £75 for dilapidation, and a further £5 per annum during his father's lifetime. This arrangement was to be kept concealed from Mr Passmore senr. The headmaster, although confined to his bed through gout, refused to resign his position, and had a window cut from his bedroom into the school, so that he could both see and hear what was taking place.

In 1849, the trustees decided that the condition of the building had deteriorated to such an extent that it should be rebuilt and tendered for the work. Four quotations were received:

*Messrs Dennis of Silverton: £297 for the School and £659 the house – a total of £956.
Mr Sharland of Silverton: £939 in total.
Mr Parish of Tiverton: £370 for the school and £570 for the house – total £940.
Mr Bater: £252 for the school and £543 for the house – total £795.*

The lowest tender from Mr Bater was accepted, but it was found that insufficient funds were available and the rebuilding of the house was postponed.

A late-19th century photograph of children in the Square, with The Richards Endowed School behind.

An infant class with teacher Annie Thomas, date unknown.

A class of girls, date unknown.

Apparently changes were continually being proposed for the rebuilding of the school, and Mr Bater did not agree to the plans so withdrew. Eventually the work was carried out by Mr Sharland. In 1850 Mr Passmore's assistant, Mr Samuel Hopkins, who had been carrying out his teaching duties, eventually succeeded him. He had trained at The Church of England Training College at Chester, and held the post until his death in 1874, when Mr John Mills

Higgins succeeded him. John Higgins died on 5 November 1879, aged 38, having made no provision for his widow. The rector and his wife, Mr and Mrs Fox-Strangways, helped her establish a private school at Berry Villa (Nettleworth House) and she continued to live at Berry Villa until Michaelmas 1907.

Only the education of the boys of Silverton has hitherto been mentioned. However, in 1730 the Revd Richard Troyte had left·

The infant class at the Girls' School, early 1900s.
Mrs Fallon is in the centre and Mrs Thomas is on the left.

Boys at the Richards Endowed School, early 1900s.

... fifty shillings yearly, for ever payable out of Netherleigh in this Parish for the putting some Poore Girles of this Parish to a Reading School who are to be nominated by the Rector, Churchwardens and Overseers.

The Charity Report of 1823 mentions a 'Reading School for Poor Girls' which was financed by voluntary subscription, and in that year almost 60 girls attended – similar to the number of boys attending the Richards School. It was recorded that the girls were taught reading, knitting and needlework. In 1847 a new school was built for girls and infants of both sexes on Glebe land by the National Society by means of a Government grant and financed by village subscriptions. Above the door an inscription declared 'Train up a child in the way he should go and when he is old he will not depart from it'.

Kelly's 1893 *Directory of Devonshire* records that the 'Endowed School will hold 100 boys', but that it had an average attendance of 75. The National School for girls and infants held 120, but had an average attendance of 103.

In addition to the charitable schools, records show that Silverton also had a number of private schools. The following report taken from the *Exeter Flying Post* dated May 14 1774 concerns one of these schools:

A Malicious Report having been industriously propagated, that Mrs Langdon is about to quit her Boarding School, at Silverton; this is to acquaint her Friends and the Public, that the report is false and without the least Foundation; that she still continues her School at her House, in an open Square called the Berry, near the Church, where young Ladies are genteely Boarded, and carefully taught all sorts of NEEDLEWORK. &c for Ten Pounds per annum.

Mrs Langdon begs leave to return her grateful thanks for the favours she has already received. And to request a continuance, as she will pay her utmost attention to the Ladies committed to her care. A Writing Master attends the School every Day - Dancing by Mr Louis of Exeter.

Boys from Richards Endowed School during the Second World War with a cup which was awarded for the highest quantity of waste paper collected for the war effort. Left to right, back row: Colin French, Fred Down, Valentine Robert*, Reg. Trump, Lawrence Skinner, Ron Palfrey, Mark Skinner, Eric Gill, Eric Gooding, Raymond Sutton, Tom Vinnicombe, Jaques Robert*, Clifford Skinner, Jean Robert*, Jimmy Webb; standing at far left: Gerald Pye, Mr Fox (headmaster); standing centre: Brian Maidment, Tom Small, Stanley Plummer (three evacuees from Barking, Essex); standing far right: Mr Dale (master), Mervyn Trump.
middle: Gordan Isaacs, Wilfred Beer, Donald Brady, Roy Williams, Jack Tree, Roy Osmond, Donald Wragg (evacuee), Peter Channon, Clive Prowse, Marcel Raspael*;
front: Henry Blee, ?, Francis Ayshford, ? Dodd, Walter Pye, Henry Dodd, Desmond Webb, Derek Stroman, Alan Price, Gilbert Dodd. NOTE: All those names marked * were French evacuees who were living at Livingshayes House at the time of the photograph.

The Girls' School in the 1890s. The teacher standing second from the left at the back is Annie Thomas. Third row: far left, Maud Ayshford and second from left, Julia Rookes.

Mr Fallon, headmaster of the Richards Endowed School, with a class of boys c.1908. The boy in the front row, fourth from left, is a young Ted Ayshford, and on his left is Frank Bastin.

The infant class, Girls' School, 1919.

The Girls' School, 1919.

Teacher Mr George Tipper with a class of boys in the late 1920s including, in the back row:
Sam Radford, Percy Carpenter, Frank Manley, Cecil Richards, Cyril Channon;
in the middle row: Jack Vittles, George Mogford, Fred Vinnicombe;
in the front row: Cecil Williams, Jack Way, George Ellis, Tom Vittles, George Brook,
Edwin Gooding, Bill Abrahams, Idris Gitsham.

Silverton Girls' School, 1928.
Left to right, back row: Winnie Hurst, Lucy Ellis, Nellie Carpenter, Violet Ball, Joan Wardle,
Joan Ellis, Lily Warren;
middle: Lavinia Priddle, Doris Lane, Edith Ball, May Mogford, Nellie Bowden, Margaret Priddle,
Mary Ellis, Doris Cudmore, Phyllis Woolway, Helen Dymond;
front, seated: Phyllis Wood, Edith Abrahams, Elizabeth Oliver, Rene Woolway.

Boys' School, 1935.
Left to right, back row: Dennis Strickland, Joe Ball, Gilbert Pearcey, ?, Noel Isaac,
Eddy Pook, Norman Beer,
middle: Bill Langabeer, Sid Langabeer, ?, Percy Brady, Arthur Fishleigh;
front: Malgwyn Rosser, Charlie Saunders, Tom Ayshford, Herbert Tulley, ?, Reg Palfrey,
Bern Ayshford.

The Richards Endowed School, 1935.
Left to right, back row: Leslie Tree, Jack Langabeer, ?, Jeffery Woolway, Percy Gooding, Tom Hill,
Reg Burgess, Wilfred E. Richards;
front: Jack Ellis, Stanley Thompson, ?, Patrick Palfrey, Wally Sussex, Leslie Woolway,
Fred Gooding, Maurice Bryant.

Boys' School, 1936. Left to right, back row: Reg Burgess, Pat Palfry, Wally Sussex, a visitor staying at Wayside, ? Woolway, ?; middle: Mick Richards, Joe Ball, Dennis Strickland, Jack Ellis, Geoff Woolway, Ray Dolling, Norman Beer; front: Maurice Bryant, Herbert Tulley, Fred Gooding, Tom Ayshford, Gilbert Pearcey.

Junior Class of Richards Endowed School, c.1938. Left to right, back row: Mr Dale (master), Ken Manning, Derek French, ?, ?, Fred Down, John Vinnicombe; middle: Peter Channon, ?, Ron Palfrey, Roy Williams, Roy Osmond, Wilf Osmond, Eric Gooding, Laurence Skinner; front: Jack Tree, Donald Short, Eric Batten, Mark Skinner, Tom Vinnicombe.

Girls' School, taken about 1949 - by that time mixed pupils.

Former Girls' School, by that time mixed, c.1951.
Left to right, back row: Miss Kerslake, Frances Brewer, Josie Gill, Angela Ball, Pauline Scott,
Christine Fry, Anne Atkinson, Colin Bennett, Mr Bunce;
middle: Mervyn Lamacraft, Antony Vittles, Jill Sinclair, Susan Vinnicombe, Terry Furbear;
front: ?, Patrick Gooding, ?, Nigel Bunce, Terry Selley, Shirley West, Barbara Trump.

A class at Silverton Primary School in 1964.
Left to right, back row: Charmaine Weeratunga, Jaqueline Burrnell, Ronald Churchill,
Janice Diamond, (student teacher?), Marion Wood, Steven French, Caroline Piney, Bruce Hamilton;
front: Michael Gill, Ann Huxtable, ?, Joy Wing, Peter Tree, Sheila Langabeer,
Michael Todd, Martin Crawford.

Silverton School, September 1981.
Left to right, back row: Michael Parnell, Sian Owen, Claire Sargent, Rachel Rice,
Mrs Helen Thomas, Robert White, Martin Westcott, Amanda Higman;
middle: Sarah Vinnicombe, Sarah Miles, Elizabeth Morse, Duncan Biggs, Michael Parker, Michael
Payne, Jane Maxwell-Hyslop, Dominique Moon, Rebecca Boxall, Christy Hooper, Diane Parkhouse;
front: Jill Liversage, Nicola Parish, Adrian Beer, Helen Sercombe, Katherine Duffy, Sally Creese,
Christopher Rolls, Andrew Ware.

Chapter 8
Parish Groups, Sports and Pastimes
A Photographic Portrait

SILVERTON FOXHOUNDS

The earliest record of the Silverton hounds is as a harrier pack in the early-18th century. They were a trencher-fed pack, run by a committee of local farmers, each of whom kept one or two couple of hounds and brought them out on hunting days. This changed in 1863 when Mr Tom Webber became Master and kennelled the hounds at Silverton where he did some serious hound breeding.

The Silverton area was typically Devonian sporting country; rough and hilly in parts with some considerable woodland. It was important to have a good 'stamp' of working hounds to hunt the country, excelling in nose, cry and perseverance. Mr Webber was Master for 32 seasons during which he bred a remarkably fine pack. In 1903 Mr Cumming became Master and this marked an important point in the evolution of the Silverton hounds as a pack of foxhounds.

In 1906 Mr Hubert Burnskill brought his own pack of foxhounds from Exmoor to hunt the Silverton country and the old Silverton harrier pack was purchased by Messrs Wilcock and Rewe. At around this time the Silverton moved to their present home at Drew's Cleave, Stoke Hill, where the pack of hounds were kennelled. The harrier pack comprised 12 couple of the old white or lemon pie and a pack of 20 couple of 21 inch foxhounds. It is recorded that good sport was shown by both packs and every support was forthcoming from the farmers. There were plenty of foxes, and in parts good hare sport. In 1911 Mr Pape took over as Master and continued for the next 16 seasons. Eventually with the outbreak of the First World War the harriers were disbanded and the Silverton then became a foxhound pack only.

There were various masters until the outbreak of the Second World War when the committee was responsible for the running of the pack. Jack Davie who was with the Silverton for 41 seasons ran the pack and hunted hounds single handed throughout the war. After the war Fred Tucker hunted hounds and Jack Davie retired. In 1947 Major R. Knight Bruce and Captain Knight Bruce took on the Mastership with Fred Tucker as first whip and kennel huntsman. Although the masters changed, Fred worked tirelessly until 1979 when he retired. The foxhounds are hunting well at the time of writing, with the present Master Mr A. J. Knox, and members of the hunt committee, Mrs P.H. Bromell, Mr R.B. Channin, Mrs S. Shere, and Dr R. Keith. The huntsman is Mr Bob Street and Chris Matterface whips in. The hounds still meet regularly in Silverton.

A meet of the Silverton Foxhounds in the 1930s.

Members of the Silverton Branch of the British Legion, prior to 1965.
Left to right, standing: Harry Quant, Gerald Barons, Ben Blackmore, Leonard Rookes, Arthur Loaring,
Mr Manley, G. Frost, Bill Dymond, Mr Dipsdale, ?, Major Campbell; seated: Fred Petherick,
Sid Withycombe, ?, ?, F. Tree, Thomas Brook, Henry Dolling, Frank Bastin, William Chudley,
Jack Thompson, Alfred Smale, William Selley, Ted Ayshford.

The ladies' section of the British Legion, 1960s. Left to right: ?, ?, Mrs Edwards, Mrs Frost,
Mrs F. Vittles, Mrs Mary Sutton, Mrs Margaret Sutton, Mrs Poole, Mrs H. Hawke, ?,
Mrs L. Hutchings, Mrs V. Vinnicombe, Mrs E. Frost, Mrs D. Heard.

Members of the Silverton branch of the Royal British Legion at a dinner held in the room behind The Three Tuns, mid to late 1950s.

A group of British Legion members at The Three Tuns, late 1940s - early '50s.

The Town Band taken on the steps of the old Girls' School, early 1900s.

The Silverton Temperance Band, c.1910.

*The Silverton Town Band, 1920s, with, left to right, back row: ?, Joseph Stocker,
Walter Abrahams, George Perratt, Walter Marsh, ?, ?;
middle row: Jimmy Yeo, Frank Ayshford, ?, John Fallon, Tommy Skinner, Charlie Yeo;
front: no names known.*

Silverton Town Band at a local function, early 1900s. The location unfortunately is unknown.

❋ Silverton Church Choir ❋

Robing of the choir, 1909. Left to right, back row: Wilfred Richards (killed 1914), Eric Tremlett, Arthur Baker, Alan Skinner, Frank Bastin; 3rd row: George Short, Bill Selley, Bill Perkins, Reg Price, Alf Manley, Leonard Yeo, Cecil Selley; 2nd row: Charlie Yeo, Walter Marsh, John Fallon, Revd Heathcote, George Short, Charlie Short, Sam Stone; front: Ted Ayshford, Percy Hayes, Monty Beer, Hector Wood.

The Silverton Church Choir outing in June 1936 to Crystal Palace where they joined choirs from throughout England to sing Handel's Messiah. The choir had been rehearsing for months under the tuition of Mrs Molineux. The group left St David's on the 10:10a.m train, and arrived at Paddington at 1:20p.m. and then went by coach or charabancs to Crystal Palace. There were hundreds of choristers participating and the event was supposed to have been broadcast by the BBC, but during the recital there was a thunderstorm that prevented the broadcast, and created much disappointment in Silverton. Crystal Palace was completely gutted by fire a few weeks later. Left to right: ?, Wilfred Richards, Walter Selley, ?, ?, Mr Turner (organist), Bill Ellis, ?, Ted. Dymond, ?, Bill Selley, Percy Hine, Percy Carpenter; boys: Joe Ball, Jack Ellis, Tom Ayshford, Frank Sutton.

Above: *Silverton Choral Society evening on Friday 24 April 1936 in the Village Hall.*

Left and below: *Front cover of the program and members' names as printed.*

THE INSTITUTE, SILVERTON

Friday, 24th April, 1936, 8 p.m.

————

SILVERTON CHORAL SOCIETY

PROGRAMME.

Choir of the Silverton Choral Society

Dr. Bradfield

Miss Pauline Passmore

Mrs. Richardson

————

Conductor : Miss Gammon, A.R.C.M.

Choral Society.

Sopranos.	Altos.
Mrs. Bryant	Miss Dowson
Mrs. Bowerman	Mrs. Finch
Mrs. Cole	Miss Gauntlett
Miss H. Dymond	Mrs. Glen
Miss K. Dymond	Mrs. Hutchings
Mrs. England	Miss Wardle
Mrs. Maddock	Mrs. Wellington
Miss Melvin	
Miss Power	
Mrs. Richardson	**Tenors.**
Mrs. Templer	Mr. Beer
Miss Vosper	Mr. Thomas
Miss Vicary	Mr. Vicary

Basses.

Rev. L. Chamberlen	Mr. Maddock
Mr. Finch	Mr. Martin
Mr. Glanville	Mr. Richardson

Captain Templer

The Excelsior Club, early 1900s.

Silverton Football Team c.1905.

Silverton United Football Team, 1907. A kind person named all the people for us at the time.

Silverton United Football Team and officials, 1920-21. Left to right, standing: Sidney Ellis, ?, Leonard Selley, ?, Walter Carpenter, Percy Frankpitt, ?, the Revd Walsh, ?, ?; front: Walter Skinner, Albert Sanders, Bill Saunders, Sidney John Hutchings (with ball), Ted Frankpitt, Bill Quick, Russell Hutchings, Mr Dymond.

Silverton United in the 1920s. Second from the left is schoolmaster John Fallon.

Silverton Football Team, 1929/30.
Left to right, back row: Bill Quick, Fred Hutchings, Jack Ware, Wilfred Kenshole, ?, ?,
Cecil Williams, Bruce Frankpitt, ?, George French, Mr Wright;
front: Bert Dymond, Ralph Hutchings, Percy Carpenter, Frank French,
Herbert Pearce.

Silverton United Football Club, 1930s. Left to right, back row: Claude Hooper, Jimmy Hutchings (Russell's father), Bill Saunders, Walter Carpenter, Alf Manley, Cecil Frost, Reg Quick; middle: Fred Gooding, Bill Quick, Percy Hine, Alec Skinner, ?; front: ?, ?, Russell Hutchings.

Silverton Football Team, late 1940s.

The unbeaten Silverton team of 1949-50 - winners of the Devon Junior Cup, the Tiverton and District League Championship, the Challenge Cup, the Walrond Cup and the Seward Cup. Left to right, back row: Victor Blatchford, Leonard Wardle, Fred Nicholson, Peter Reynolds, Harry Bulley, Jimmy Dymond; front: Russell Hutchings, Jack Rosser, Jack Haydon, Reg Rutley, Charlie Saunders.

Silverton United Football Team, 1959-60. Left to right, back row: R. Condon, K. Vinnicombe, J. Knight, B. Gooding, J. Furbear, C. Manley, A. Underhill, W. Skinner; front: E. Bryant, T. Hitchcock, P. Pinhey, T. Gooding, E. Gill, D. German, L. Skinner.

❋ Charity Football ❋

Charity Football Team.
Left to right, standing: Nick Mogford, Don Strath, Terry Selly, Reith Roberts, Colin Green, Mike Shapcott, Eric Clark, Peter Crabtree, ?, Jack Rosser, Eric Piney, Father George Hodgshon (referee), Bussey Carpenter, Don Lopez, Garth Sanders, Dave Piney, ?, ?, David Courtney-Stamp; front: Basil Sharland, ?, ?; kneeling: Peter Boundy, Ray Westcott, Jim Turner, Tony Vittles, John Frankpitt, and, hidden, Eric Turner.

Charity Football Team.
Left to right: Dave Piney, Ray Westcott, Eric Piney, Bussey Carpenter, Jack Rosser, ?, Father George Hodgshon (referee), Basil Sharland, Don. Strath, Peter Crabtree, Don. Lopez, ?, David Courtney-Stamp, ?, ?, ?.

Silverton Rugby Team, early 1900s.

The bowling club prize-giving at the Rectory. Left to right: Mr Frank Ayshford,
William Valentine, Jack Thompson, Mr Hooper, ?, Alfred Vinnicombe, ?, ?, ?, Tom Vittles,
Mrs Heathcote, ?, ?, ?, George French, Jack Abrahams, Reverend Heathcote, ?.

Silverton Women's Institute, early-20th century.

Women's Institute outing in a Greenslade's Charabanc, in the 1920s. (Note the solid tyres!)

❀ Mother's Union ❀

The Silverton Mother's Union AGM at Wayside on 14 July 1976. Left to right: Mrs Sercombe, Mrs Eileen Stradling, Mrs Joan Frankpitt, Mrs Moore, Miss Drury, Mrs Ann Watson (rector's wife), Mrs Pam Parsons, Mrs Daisy Tree. (J.V. Swain)

The Silverton Mother's Union Tea Party and AGM, 14 July 1976. (J.V. Swain)
Left to right, standing: Mrs P. Vinnicombe, Mrs Sercombe, Mrs Cole, Mrs C. Gooding, Mrs Vicary, Mrs Haycraft, Mrs Hodgshon, Mrs Rooke, Mrs Sharland, Mrs L. Frankpitt, Mrs E. Hodgson, Mrs E. Stradling, Revd A. Watson, Mrs D. Tree, Mrs Watkins, Mrs Turner, Mrs Watson, Mrs Barons, Mrs Harwood, Mrs P. Piney, Mrs P. Parsons;
seated: Mrs Faulkner, Mrs S. Hallett, Mrs Shere, Mrs Shenton, Mrs Ayshford, Miss Drury, Mrs Tremlett, Mrs Edwards, Mrs E. Frost, Mrs Piney, Mrs J. Frankpitt;
children: babe in arms Sarah Vinnicombe, Helen Sercombe, Ricky Sercombe, Philip Gooding, Robert Barons, Andrew Parsons, Caroline Parsons, Christine Parsons, Julie Barons, Clare Parsons.

A party arranged for Silverton's senior citizens in the early 1950s.

A locally produced concert party in the New Hall for senior citizens, 1957. The ballerinas at the front were gentlemen of the village including, second from right, Bill 'Bussy' Carpenter. Others known include: Mrs Vittles, Mrs Heard, Mrs Hilton, Mrs Brookes, Mrs Nicholson, Mrs Hawke, Mrs Skinner, Mrs Tree, Mrs Frost, Mrs Gooding and Mrs Boundy.

❁ Village Outings ❁

Left: *Outing of Silverton residents in the 1920s.*

Right: *An outing organised by The Lamb Inn. Included in the back row are: L. Valentine, S. Hutchings, F. Tree (junr), C. Munkley, F. Vinnicombe, W. Selley, J. Kenshole, G. Barons; left to right, front: G. Wardle, W. Marsh (landlord), V. Valentine, J. Brady, J. Thompson, ?, F. Blatchford, S. Dart, W. Tree, G Tree, F. Tree senr.*

Left: *RAOB (Royal Antediluvian Order of Buffaloes) outing to Wells and Cheddar, 1938.*

Below: *Church choir outing to Cheddar, in 1932.*

Chapter 9
War Memorial
and HMS *Silverton*

The War Memorial

During the summer of 1935 Laetitia Chalk (daughter of the Revd J.H. Ward, rector of Silverton, from 1894 to 1909) returned to Silverton where she looked at the war memorial in the Square. Reading the inscription she remarked that it:

... was like recalling her Sunday School roll over again. The boys all joined up together at the beginning of the war and quite a few of them were killed by the same German shell while sheltering in a barn. The first to lose his life was Charlie Hayes of the Flock Mill, my fellow teacher, who went down on the first ship torpedoed by the enemy. The last to who I bade farewell at Exeter Station was Ted Read, the chubby little boy who walked beside me coming out of Church.

I should not think that any other place of it's size lost as many as Silverton. In that war they all were volunteers, as in a crusade. It was a war to end all wars, and build up a world for heroes to live in. Over the years many must have looked at the names on the war memorial, and the plaque inside St Mary's Church, and wondered about the men whose names are recorded, who joined the forces never again to return to their Silverton home. Great sadness must have been felt by all, and there could have been no one that did not lose a close relative or friend.

HMS *Silverton/Krakowiak*

1939–46, Hunt Class Destroyer, 1430-ton displacement, speed 25 knots.

The Hunts, of which 86 were built, were cheap, easily constructed, 'utility' destroyers. They were all named after well-known hunts such as Eggesford, Exmoor, Tetcott, Beaufort, Stevenstone, etc. Almost half of these hard-working ships were substantially damaged or sunk during their war service, the majority by mines or air attack.

HMS *Silverton* was transferred to the Polish Navy in 1941, operating in the 15th Destroyer Flotilla at

HMS Silverton

Plymouth, and renamed 'Krakowiak'. Between 22 December 1941 and 1 November 1942 she formed part of the escort for the raiding force in the Lofoten Islands. On 17 June 1942 *Krakowiak*, with the destroyers *Wild Swan* and *Beagle* and the frigate *Spey*, was part of the support group sent to aid convoy HG84. The group was itself attacked by aircraft and *Wild Swan* was lost. Four months later *Krakowiak*, with *Fernie*, *Tynedale* and *Brocklesby*, was in action against German torpedo boats near Cap de la Hague on the night of 13/14 October 1942, and again on 5 May 1943 whilst protecting a convoy off Start Point, when she drove off attacking MTBs.

In June 1943 *Krakowiak* sailed for the Mediterranean where she stayed for the next ten months acting as an escort for the invasion of Italy. With *Petard* and *Rickwood* she shelled Calino on 11 November 1943, and 17 days later attended the cruiser *Birmingham* after that vessel had been torpedoed on passage from Gibraltar to the Levant.

Returning to the United Kingdom in 1944, *Krakowiak* took part in the 'D' Day Landings, and was officially handed back to the Royal Navy as HMS *Silverton* in September 1946. She remained in service in the Reserve Fleet and attended the Coronation Revue in 1953. On 11 March 1958 HMS *Silverton* was approved for scrapping, and a year later was towed to the scrapyard of Thos. W. Ward at Grays for a price recorded as £17 400.

First World War

Surname	Christian N.	Rank	Regiment	Details
Abrahams	Henry	Private	Worcestershire Regiment	Son of James & Ann Abraham. Died 14th. June 1916 at Pas de Calais, France
Adams	Edward W.	Private	4th. Canadian Brigade	No details known
Anley	James	Private	Devonshire Regiment	Died 18th. November 1914 at Ypres, Belgium
Ball	John	Private	Durham Lt. Inf.	Husband of Jenny of Lease Cottages Hele. Died at the Battle of Mons.
Carpenter	Frederick S.	Private	Devonshire Regiment	Died 9th. November 1916 at The Somme
Channon	Reginald	Private	Worcestershire Regiment	Son of Frank and Fanny Charnon of Parsonage Lane. Died 13th. April 1918 Aged 19 at Flanders
Combeer	John Llewellyn	Private	Devonshire Regiment	Died 31st. October 1914 at Pas de Calais
Davey	Ernest	Gunner	Devonshire Regiment	Died 17th. June 1916 in Mesopotamia, Iraq.
Davey	Samuel J.	Private	Canadians	No details known
Dawe	William H.	Private	Coldstream Guards	No details known
Dredge	Llewellyn	Private	1st. Essex	Son of Lavinia Dredge of Chard. Died 6th. August 1915 aged 26 in Turkey.
Fox Strangways	Theodore	Major	Royal Irish Rifles	Son of Rev. Henry Fox-Strangways, Rector of Silverton. Died 19th. March 1917 Aged 54 in France.
Goodwin	Reginald John	Private	Royal Marines	Son of Thomas & Emily Goodwin Latchmoor Cottages Thorverton. Died 12th. April 1916 at Gallipoli
Haydon	Leonard George	Private	Coldstream Guards	Son of John & Emily Haydon of The High Street. Died 19th. September 1914. Age 24 in Northern France.
Hayes	Charles	A B	Royal Navy	Died 1st. November 1914 on HMS *Monmouth*
Hooper	Cecil Herbert	Sergeant	Duke of Cornwall Lt. Inf.	Son of Minard G. & Francis A. Hooper of Hillside. Died 9th. March 1918. Aged 24 in India
Kenshole	Ernest A.	Private	Royal Berkshire	Son of William & Henrietta Kenshole of Parsonage Lane. Died 8th. October 1918 aged 19 at Nord, France
Kenshole	William J.	Private	Hampshire	Brother of Ernest. Died in France 1st. December 1918 aged 18
Lipscombe	Harry	Private	Duke of Cornwall Lt. Inf.	Nephew of Jane Valentine of High Street. Died 3rd. September 1918 aged 41 in Greece.
Long	John	Private	Devonshire Regiment	Son of John & Hannah Long of Broadclyst. Died 7th. December 1916 aged 33 in Greece.
Matthews	Henry	Private	Royal Marine Lt. Inf.	No details known
Moore	Edward Westbrooke	Sergeant	Royal Marine Artillery	Husband of Rose of Church Terrace. Died in France.
Murch	Ernest Arthur	Private	Devonshire Regiment	Son of John & Emma Murch of Ellerhayes. Died 26th. April 1918 aged 24 at The Somme.
Murch	Frederick G.	Private	Worcestershire Regiment	Brother of Ernest. Died at Ypres 10th. April 1918 aged 22.
Nesham	Henry John	Private	Life Guards	Son of Charles Courtnay & Eliz. Nesham of Torquay. Died 10th. October 1918 aged 28 at The Somme.
Pye	William Way	Private	Devonshire Regiment	Died 24th. December 1914 at Ypres.
Read	Edward Macartney	Lieut.	Devonshire Regiment	Son of William Macartney & Ellen Read of Livingshayes. Died 2nd. April 1917 aged 27 at Pas de Calais France.

CONT.

First World War Continued

Surname	Christian N.	Rank	Regiment	Details
Read	Thomas Jaffray	Lance Corporal	South African Infantry	Brother of Edward. Died 1st. August 1916 aged 33 at The Somme
Richards	Wilfred Ernest	Private	Devonshire Regiment	From Fore Street. Died 7th. October 1916 aged 19 at The Somme.
Rookes	William John	Lance Corporal	Devonshire Regiment	Son of Sam. & Eliz. Rookes husband of Ellen of Church Terrace. Died 31st. October 1916 aged 31 at The Somme.
Sanger	William George	Air Mechanic	Royal Flying Corps.	Died 26th. March 1918 at Pas de Calais.
Sellick	Walter J.	Private	Bedfordshire	Died 7th. May 1915 at Ypres.
Slade	George Thomas	Corporal	20th. Hussars	Son of Peter & Sarah Slade of Park Gardens. Died 26th. March 1918 Aged 31 at The Somme.
Sutton	Charles William	Private	Devonshire Regiment	Son of Mrs. Sarah Sutton of Greenslinch. Died 26th. October 1917. Age 21 at Ieper Belgium.
Tree	James	Driver	R F A	Died in France.
Vittles	William	Private	Devonshire Regiment	Husband of Emily & Father of eight. Died 15th. February 1917 at Pas de Calais France.
Vosper	George Francis	Chief Boatswain	Royal Navy	Son of George & Eliza Vosper husband of late Eliza. Died 16th. April 1915 Age 47 On HMS *Powerful*
Wills	Tom	Driver	R F A	No details known
Yeo	John	Private	Devonshire Regiment	Died 11th. March 1915 at Pas de Calais.

Second World War

Surname	Christian N.	Rank	Regiment	Details
Ball	Joseph			
Bowen	Charles	Private	1st. Btn. Devonshire	Son of James & Mary Bowen. Farm worker from Ellerhayes. Died 27th. August, 1943, aged 26 in India.
Clapp	Frank	Able Seaman	Royal Navy	Husband of Florence Clapp, of King Street. Died 24th. July, 1941 on HMS *Fearless*.
Clements	Lionel	N/K	N/K	From Coach Road. Army Despatch Rider. Killed in Action
Crispen	William	Private	Army Service Corps	Son of Henry & Mary Crispin of Ellerhayes. Captured at St. Valery in France. Died 22nd. February, 1941, aged 24, in POW camp in Poland.
Cuddehay	Clarence George	Flight Sergeant	RAF	Son of James & Hannah Cuddehay; husband of Ivy. Died 20th. April, 1945, aged 45.
Furbear	Thomas George	Sergeant	Royal Marines	Son of William & Edith Furbear, husband of Gertrude. Died 14th. October, 1939, aged 32, on HMS *Royal Oak* at Scapa Flow.
Gooding	Percy	Private	Army, West Kent Regiment	Son of Ernest & Eliz. Gooding, of Coach Road. Died in Italy, 6th. July, 1944. Age 23
Pine	William Henry	Petty Officer	Royal Navy	Son of William & Sarah Pine. Died 22nd. October, 1946, aged 28, on HMS *Saumarez* when it hit a mine after the end of hostilities.
Salter	Arthur	Trooper	18th Regt. Reconnaissance Corps	Died 9th. March, 1943 in Japanese POW Camp in Thailand (Siam) Aged 36. Son of W. & E Salter of Livingshayes Road.
Warren	Reginald	Fire Service	Royal Navy	Killed in Plymouth Blitz.

Mrs Christine Higgins with girls at the Berry Villa School.

Berry Villa, a school for young ladies in the early 1900s.
Mrs Higgins, Principal, between two pupils.

Chapter 10
Silverton Characters – Near and Far

ARTHUR AND ALBERT HOPKINS

Mr Samuel Hopkins (*right*) was appointed headmaster of the Richards Endowed School on 2 January 1850, having for some years acted as assistant head. His wife the former Anna Margarita Phelps Richards is believed to be the great-granddaughter of Charles Richards, younger brother of John, the benefactor of the school. Although born at Porlock, the coincidence of her husband's appointment resulted in Anna returning to the parish that for four centuries at least had been the home of her family.

While living at Silverton Anna gave birth to five children, Arthur Richards Phelps Hopkins, William Richards, Henrietta, William Richards and Alfred. The name William proved unlucky as the first born died in infancy, and the other was to die in 1878 at the age of 17, while bathing in the River Thames.

Arthur became an apprentice, and later mate, on tea-clippers. He served aboard the famous *Thermopylae*, one time rival of the *Cutty Sark*. While still a mariner he was in charge of a recruiting schooner for the Queensland sugar plantations, and during one voyage visited Auckland, New Zealand. Here Arthur decided to settle, although he eventually travelled south to Christchurch, where he became manager for 20 years of a frozen meat company. After retiring he lived on a citrus fruit farm, and it was from here in 1907 that he wrote to the vicar at Silverton after obtaining several copies of the *Devon & Exeter Gazette*. One of these contained an account of the Silverton Flower Show, and he wrote:

... reading this with the old familiar boyhood days names, my heart is full and old memories crowd around me. Read, Savery, Walland, Farmer, Dymond, Haydon and many others.

I have a very fine photograph of the old church and often look at it and tell my boys of the long-ago days when the eight o'clock bell used to ring on Sunday mornings. I have never heard such a beautiful tone in any bell since; I do not believe there is another like it in this world. An English Sabbath Day in summer and the long delightful twilight walks, one down the Poundsland road to the farmhouse then occupied by my Uncle Mr Robert Dewdney, across the fields to the Mill over the bridge and up the meadow to Hayne Barton and so by the lane home. Hedges full of primroses, violets and wild flowers of every description, what a wealth of blossom and perfume and it is thirty years ago. Another past Rippells shop on the right and Mr Robt. Webber's on the left, down the lane to the Tiverton road, and so across the fields to the River Exe. Ah the dear old County! There are quite a large number of Devonshire men settled here and we all love it so (Besley, Coplestones, Treavilles, Chamberlins, Cliffords, Aclands, Radfords, Haydon, Northcote, Edworthys, Carews and many others). When we meet at saleyards and any public function a warm clasp of the hand and the usual query 'Heard from Home lately?' Home, 16 000 miles away!

When I lived in Silverton my people lived at Berry House, my Uncle Dewdney occupied Poundsland, Uncle Player had Balls Farm, my Grandfather owned The Poplars on the Jenny's Portion road. Lady Egremont still held court at old Silverton House, Mr Read's farm was on the hill above the Rectory and Mr Strangways reigned at the latter. If I have one unfulfilled ambition in life it is to go home once more, be again a boy of 13, and again rob the great cherry tree at the Rectory.

Arthur Hopkins died in 1938 after returning again to Auckland. His brother Alfred also joined him in New Zealand where he was regimental sergeant major in the Volunteer Canterbury Regiment. For many years manager of a retail business, one of Alfred's many interests was the Scout movement, for which he received an award from Lord Baden-Powell. Neither brother is known to have returned to his birthplace, but both have many descendants in New Zealand, some of whom have visited Silverton, and are proud of their Devonian heritage.

An artist's impression of Silverton Rectory c.1850, the home that Charles Tripp departed from to emigrate to New Zealand.

The property at Orari Gorge that is still occupied by the Tripp family. It was built for Charles Tripp, mainly by Jim Radford, the stonemason from Silverton. Jim married and settled at Temuka in South Island, where his descendants still live. (G. Pauley)

TRIPP AND ACLAND

Charles George Tripp was the third son of the Revd Dr Charles Tripp, vicar of Silverton from 1838 until 1865. Having studied at Merchant Taylor's School in London, Charles then worked for five years in an estate business and on a Hampshire Farm. During 1850 he approached his father with a plan to emigrate to New Zealand and start a sheep farm, but the Revd was totally opposed to this idea. Charles was persuaded to study law, which he commenced in 1851. After three years he was called to the Bar. However, being a London lawyer was not to Charles' liking, and he longed for a life in the country.

Law was also the chosen career of another from the Silverton area, John Barton Acland, the sixth son of Sir Thomas and Lady Lydia Dyke Acland of Killerton. Charles and John became close friends and discussed Charles' dream to travel to New Zealand. Their families were approached and although both actively discouraged the venture, they eventually reluctantly agreed. The two men, who were aged 29 and 32, travelled on the 'Royal Stuart' from London for New Zealand with their dream of producing the 'the best of England in the Antipodes'. Tripp had planned well and travelled with many supplies, which included £200 worth of boots including ladies' fashionable pairs made of leather – also ploughs, grindstones, a Whitechapel cart, 12 saddles, harnesses, tarpaulins, axes, pickaxes, cement, arsenic, brandy, gin, wine and 15 000 bricks, much of which he intended to sell when they arrived.

The voyage lasted almost three months and on 4 January 1855 the two Devonians arrived at Lyttelton, the port of Christchurch in South Island. Tripp's goods were sold profitably, especially the ladies' boots which were much in demand! This income enabled them to purchase two horses and travel around the Canterbury Plains, watching and learning from the settlers who had already colonised the area. Unfortunately they soon became disillusioned as they found that all the areas suitable for sheep farming had already been settled.

Charles was of the opinion that land thought to be a wilderness on the lower slopes of the hills could be cleared and stocked, so they travelled further south and at an area they later named Forest Creek set fire to the valley sides. In four hours they had burnt 50 000 acres of wilderness, and after three days of fierce fires the land for ten miles around was cleared. This action was continued for three weeks – the men travelling, burning and scattering grass seed before they returned to Christchurch.

Two months later they again travelled, visiting the gorge that they called Ashburton, and two lakes that they named Tripp and Acland. Surprisingly, nowhere in the new territory seems to have been named after their homes of Silverton and Killerton.

After returning again to Christchurch a number of mainly ewe lambs were purchased, and eight bullocks with yokes, together with other equipment needed to initially carry the baggage and materials south, and later to work the land. Four men were employed to help, plus a married couple named Robert and Elizabeth Smith who had travelled from Shropshire some years earlier on the *Cressy*, one of the four ships that brought the original settlers that colonised New Zealand.

After travelling for more than a fortnight towards the south, John and Charles arrived at their chosen area to build the settlement that was later named Mount Peel. A house was constructed of wood from the bush, with a thatched roof similar to the cottages in their Silverton home. An out-station for the men to live in was also built, and a kitchen garden dug to provide vegetables to supplement the food that had been brought from Christchurch, and meat from locally-killed wild pigs.

During December a vessel arrived at Lyttelton from England. Amongst the passengers was a vicar from the Parish of Stratfield Mortimer, near Reading. The Revd Henry John Chitty Harper was accompanied by his wife, their four sons and six daughters. Two of these girls would later become the wives of Charles and John. On Christmas Day 1856 the Revd Harper was enthroned as the Bishop of Christchurch, at a service attended by many settlers including Charles Tripp.

During March 1857 John Acland returned to England, to give a report on their success to his family and friends. Ten bales of wool had been sold to London, and, with Mount Peel stocked with four thousand sheep, their future prospects looked good. While John was in England, Charles married Ellen Harper, and after his return in the following year, John married Ellen's sister Emily. While in New Zealand both men sent many letters home to England, including one from John Acland that was prepared for the *Bath and West Agricultural Journal* in 1858. These letters were to act as an advertisement to persuade others to emigrate, which is well illustrated today by the number of New Zealanders searching for their ancestors in Devonian parishes.

Acland and Tripp continued to extend the estate by purchasing and clearing more land, but in 1862 it was decided that the partnership should be dissolved. The land was shared, and it was decided by the toss of a coin that John Acland should retain Mount Peel, and Charles have Orari Gorge.

In October 1862 Charles, Ellen and their children sailed from Lyttelton to Melbourne where they stayed with Charles' cousin, Mrs William Upton Tripp, who had established the first girls' school in the city. On 17 December they sailed from

Melbourne for England, as news had reached Charles of his father's ill health that had resulted in his total blindness. The voyage to Weymouth lasted 72 days and on reaching Silverton, the large stone building that was Silverton Vicarage amazed the children. This property, later to be known as Prispen House, was vastly different from anything they had seen previously in New Zealand or Australia. They spent over a year in England, but this was the last time that Charles would see his parents as his father died on 9 April 1865 (and is buried in Silverton churchyard). His mother Francis died the next year on 4 April and is buried at Brendon, North Devon, where her son-in-law, the Revd J.H. Wise, was rector.

While in Silverton, Charles gave a lecture to the villagers in the Parish Hall describing the sea voyage and his and John Acland's life on the other side of the world. This talk so impressed three young men that they accompanied the Tripps when they sailed back the following year. These were George Hammond, who became a ploughman, Jim Radford, a mason, and a butcher named Frank Hopkins, the son of William Hopkins, for many years a butcher in the village.

Charles and his family sailed in April 1864 on the *Ivanhoe* taking with them many supplies that would not be available in New Zealand including new straps, buckles and travelling cases that they had had made by J. Talbott the Silverton saddler. Also a cow was purchased, and taken on the voyage from Plymouth. This proved to be fortuitous, as this journey were far worse than they had previously experienced. The fresh milk was shared with other families who were suffering as a result of the rotten food and poor conditions that led to the death of 26 people from typhoid fever. On their eventual arrival at Lyttelton, the *Ivanhoe* was quarantined for a week, and the Captain was charged at the Magistrates Court. However, before the case concluded, he drank a bottle of brandy and was found drowned in Lyttelton Harbour.

Life in New Zealand was certainly not easy but the two Devonians persevered, and are remembered as pioneering settlers of the sheep farming that was to make the hills of South Canterbury famous the world over. Charles Tripp died on 6 July 1897, aged 71, and is buried at Woodbury Cemetery, Canterbury. John Acland died on 18 May 1904 and lies in the graveyard of the small church that he built at Mount Peel in 1868. They are remembered by descendants, some of whom have returned to their Silverton roots, as can be seen by entries in the visitor's book at St Mary's Church.

A Devonian travelling in this part of New Zealand would recognise many names such as Ashburton and Woodbury but would not be aware that other items originated in Devon. Many species of plants and trees were purchased from the nurseries of Veitch at Exeter, especially both eating apples and varieties that were used to make cider at the Tripp's home, Orari Gorge.

Killerton House. The home that John Barton Acland left, to seek his fortune in New Zealand.

ARCHIE TREMLETT

Born in Silverton in December 1891, Archie was baptised at St Mary's Church by the Revd Henry Fox-Strangways on 24 February 1892. Archie's brother, Henry, who was 16 months older, was also christened at the same ceremony. The two boys, and later a third brother Ernest, were sons of Sidney and Bessie Tremlett. Sidney was a Silverton blacksmith at his forge in Tiverton Road, as was his father Robert.

In 1893 the family moved from their cottage beside the forge after it was damaged by fire. A relative, James Potter, and his wife Jemima, were running The Three Tuns, and Sidney was soon to combine running the inn with his trade as blacksmith. The pub was home for both businesses until the 1920s.

During the First World War Henry and Ernest joined the Navy, and this remained their career throughout the war and the inter-war periods. During the Second World War, Henry became Chief Petty Officer on submarines and Ernest a Captain. Archie joined the Devon Yeomanry, and after the end of hostilities returned to his native Silverton to become the third generation blacksmith in the village – not that Archie was any ordinary smith, for his standards were so high that in 1937 he won the silver medal for the best shod horse in the farriers' class at Devon County Show.

Archie was a popular character and regularly followed the hunt with his terrier dogs. These were a common sight following him as he peddled his bicycle around the village. A talent of Archie's was the charming of warts, but this was accomplished with no ceremony, purely by looking at them. People would visit him from villages throughout the area for this service, for which he would not accept payment as he believed that this would diminish his powers. Dentistry was another of Archie's services and one which was normally carried out in one of the village pubs, when he would oblige the toothache sufferer by removing the offending tooth with a pair of pliers!

Archie remained a bachelor, although he apparently courted a young lady from Rewe for many years. However, he would not leave his beloved Silverton to live in the Exe Valley, and she refused to climb the hill to Silverton! A custom of Archie's was to give every newborn baby in the parish a gift of half-a-crown, a perhaps unexpected gesture for a bachelor.

After his death in 1973, the forge became derelict, a situation to which the Silverton WI drew attention. Archie's nephew, Harry S.G. Tremlett, agreed to present the building complete with all of the many tools and equipment, to the Tiverton Museum. Photographs were taken and the forge with its contents was dismantled, cleaned and removed to Tiverton where it is now displayed as a lasting tribute to a man who was one of the great characters of Silverton.

Top: *Archie Tremlett shoeing a pony in his smithy.*
Above: *Archie Tremlett enjoying a pint at The Three Tuns with the landlord Richard Baron, c.1970.*
(P. Crabtree)

❁ Silverton Station ❁

Left: *Silverton Station from the Exeter direction. The Bristol and Exeter Railway was opened for passengers on 1 May, 1844, but Silverton Station was not opened until 1867.*

Right: *Annie Langdon, Silverton stationmaster's daughter in her pony and trap, with the observatory in the background.*

Below: *A photograph of Silverton Station taken before the line was altered to narrow gauge in 1892. Note the greenhouse on the platform!*

Below: *A train travelling towards Exeter in the 1950s. The leading coach of the 'Flying Dutchman' was derailed close to Silverton on 24 May 1876, as it travelled west. Luckily due to the speed being less than 60 m.p.h., there was only minor damage, the coupling broke and the remaining carriages came to rest on the up line.*

Above: *The stationmaster's house, showing R. Langdon's observatory in the garden.*

ROGER LANGDON: SILVERTON'S ASTRONOMER STATIONMASTER

Roger Langdon, known as the 'Peasant Astronomer', was born in the village of Chisleborough, Somerset, on 22 April, 1825. The son of the parish clerk, with nine brothers and sisters, Roger had very little formal education and was taught basic reading and writing by his mother, using only a slate. By the age of seven his future love of making things was already being displayed, when he produced copies of Punch and Judy characters (that he had seen at a show in Chisleborough) from turnips! At eight he began working for a local farmer, Joseph Greenham, but after enduring four years labouring in all weathers, and being bullied by 'Jim the ploughman', he saved a pound and walked to Weymouth. From here Roger sailed to Jersey, where he lived for eight years, working in various trades including that of blacksmithing, before returning to England.

In his mid twenties Roger became engaged to Ann Warner of Henley-on-Thames, and in 1850 began working for the Bristol and Exeter Railway as a porter on Bristol Station. After their marriage, Roger became a railway policeman, and then a signalman at Stoke Canon, where he and Ann lived at an inn called the King's Arms Inn during 1851. Whilst here Ann taught at a local school to supplement Roger's wages.

In 1854 he was moved to Martock in Somerset, and then transferred to nearby Durston as a switchman. Although only paid a wage of £1 for a working day that started at 6.00a.m. and finished at 10.00p.m., Roger found the time to make his first telescope. In 1865 he was moved to Taunton and, finally, in 1867, he was appointed stationmaster at Silverton Station, where his family moved to join him in their new home. Here he remained until retiring in 1890 at the age of 65.

How Roger first became interested in astronomy is not known, but although he worked single-handed at Silverton for long hours each day, he resumed making telescopes. With one of these he was able to view the rings of Saturn, and in 1872 lectured to the Royal Astronomical Society in London on the markings of Venus, a subject on which he wrote two papers.

After selling one of his telescopes for £10, Roger found himself with enough money to commence building his own observatory in the garden of Station House. This was a circular cast-iron structure, with a conical shaped revolving roof, and two opening flaps through which to observe the sky. From this building he photographed the stars and planets (an amazing achievement for an amateur in the 19th century), recorded the path of the planet Venus, and drew over 1000 sketches of the moon's surface. In 1874 he made a plaster model of the visible hemisphere of the surface of the moon, detailing 500 principal objects, hollows, craters, and mountains, and this he presented to the Devon and Exeter Institution where apparently it still remains. He built his own portable darkroom, and his many interesting working models including one of Stoke Canon Church, from which a peal of bells that imitated those in the church could be heard when a coin was inserted.

To supplement Roger's income, and support their family of eight children, Ann Langdon again taught. After work Roger would go to his workshop near the house, where in addition to the telescopes he also made a camera with which he became one of the first to photograph the Flying Dutchman, which he accomplished as it sped through Silverton Station. Richard John, their third son, also joined the railway company and became his father's successor at Silverton as stationmaster from 1890 until 1925.

Roger Langdon became a great friend of Sir Thomas Dyke Acland, and on his death on 18 July 1894, aged 69, Sir Thomas gave permission for Roger to be buried in the churchyard of the Acland's private chapel on the Killerton Estate at Columb John. His wife Ann, and two of their sons, are also buried here.

The west-bound platform at Silverton, with a passenger train travelling towards London.

GENERAL PRACTITIONERS IN SILVERTON

The Devon and Exeter Hospital was founded in 1741. However, Silverton's earliest medical record comes from property deeds dated 1834 which show Dr Elias Puddicombe, tenant of Cockhaynes (Wayside) practising 'Medicine Surgery' in Silverton and the surrounding district. In the 1851 census Dr Elias Puddicombe, aged 52, and his nephew Edward M. Puddicombe, aged 30, were both listed as G.Ps. Dr Puddicombe brought Arthur Hopkins into the world at Berry Villa (Nettleworth) in 1858.

The 1881 census shows Dr Edward Puddicombe, a surgeon and MRCS aged 61, living at Cockhaynes with a housekeeper and two servants. His son Edward Leonard, aged 15, was a boarder at Blundells school. Deeds of 1892 place Dr Ernest Lionel Puddicombe as living at Rose Cottage (Pembridge Cottage), Tiverton Road. Finally, the deeds of Poplar House (The White House), Tiverton Road, dated November 1892, show Dr Edward Leonard Puddicombe, Surgeon, aged 25, taking out a mortgage on the house. Thus the Puddicombe family served the village in this capacity for about 60 years.

In 1904 Dr Owen Clayton Jones, MB Oxon, and his wife came to Silverton and lived at Silverton House. He was the GP for 23 years, and a tribute in the *Western Times* on his death on 7 March 1927 shows him to be a memorable doctor: the rector, the Revd Heathcote, said in his sermon that Dr Clayton Jones' cleverness and kindness had made a deep impression on the village.

The doctor was never seen at church on Sunday mornings because he was visiting his patients, but on Sunday evenings he was always present. During the whole time that he was in Silverton he had never taken a holiday. Such men, by the nobility of their character, turned the drudgery of labour into a holiday. Ron Bowerman recalls:

As a child I remember the doctor with his white beard stopping to give children a ride in his three-wheeler car. Kids would be perched everywhere, waving gleefully to those not able to get on. Until he acquired this car in 1920 he had had to do his rounds on horseback.

Ron also remembers the doctor ordering straw to be laid on the road outside the Bowerman's house, when his mother was very ill in order to deaden the sound of passing vehicles.

Dr Clayton Jones was 70 when he died, and his stone in Silverton churchyard bears the inscription: 'For 23 years an untiring worker in this Parish'. His wife was a member of the Royal Academy and has painted some wonderful pictures of Silverton, which will hopefully hang again in the village one day.

HEDERMAN STORY

Dr Patrick and Mrs Lily Hederman.

In 1926 a 'larger than life' Irishman arrived in Silverton which must have been quite a change from working in the Sea Mission in Port Talbot. He acquired his house from the previous incumbent, Dr Clayton Jones, in the centre of the village, and with his wife, embarked on the care of the sick from the same place for the next 40 years. He loved the country. His family had connections with horses and perhaps Silverton was not such an unfamiliar habitat for him.

His early professional life predated most modern medicines. His patients were recruited from those that could afford private fees and the working men who had registered under the State panel system. This entitled them to free care when they were ill, and Dr Hederman to an annual fee to include the cost of medicines. Their families were not covered. Various 'Friendly Societies' such as the Rechabites and the Buffaloes accepted a regular payment in return for sickness cover. Admission to hospital was extremely rare and often regarded as a 'one-way trip' by the patient. The staff at the hospital was limited to a few visiting specialists - the first gynaecologist/ obstetrician had yet to be appointed.

Thus, a highly competent doctor began a long career looking after a village with an assistant and his loyal wife. Ultimately he would be replaced by a team of doctors, nurses and other professionals numbering about 25 and providing over 12 000 consultations a year, part of a group of 20 practices purchasing care for 100 000 patients.

It is hard to imagine practice before the last war - in the days before antibiotics. With every woman giving birth at home, most of the doctor's night calls related to home deliveries, occasionally having to attend a mother in trouble and supervise both anaesthetic with chloroform whilst also helping a new villager into the world. It is a tribute to his skills that in such a long career, only one woman died in labour. Her case was beyond the skills of any doctor in those days.

Pneumonia could kill. Common enough amongst the frail or malnourished it would reach a crisis by the ninth day at which point the chances of survival could be relatively accurately predicted. Hederman could do little but support a grieving family and, with some misgivings, prescribe some of the then fashionable remedies, such as strychnine injections or mustard poultices to the chest! The arrival of the aniline dye derivatives – early sulphonamides – were a godsend with some genuine antibiotic activity. Although occasionally prone to dye the patient blue, at least recovery would be the more dramatic! Penicillin was slow to arrive in Silverton being much needed at the war front. It was nauseating and Dr Hederman had one third bottles of champagne made up by Gilbeys to ease the medicine down – for those that could afford it of course. Penicillin injections were painful and in spite of the content for some odd reason often gave rise to small abscesses at the site of injection.

During the war the practice was joined by Dr Avis Blundell-Jones who stayed on until the birth of her second child in 1949. She came from a busy snowbound practice in the Midlands to be near her husband, then a surgical registrar (later a very well known consultant orthopaedic surgeon in Exeter). She recalled the pleasure of arriving in Devon with its glorious countryside, full of colour even in winter, to meet the local doctor with what at first seemed a baffling Irish accent!

Dr Hederman in his dispensary.

The clouds of war hung over the valley then; the distant sounds of naval gunfire, the Blitz that hit Exeter and the many American soldiers practising for the Normandy landings. At a time of rationing and austerity, the Americans' arrival caused a stir of excitement, especially across the river in Thorverton where a contingent with all of their vehicles was billeted. A first-rate professional relationship was cemented from the very start by the happy outcome of Avis' first home visit to a case of meningitis which she immediately admitted to hospital. Other examples of her skill established her reputation in spite of the inevitable prejudice from some towards women doctors in those days. Dr Blundell-Jones says that her years in partnership with Dr Hederman were the happiest of her career.

Dr Hederman's predecessor had ridden a horse to get around the practice until in 1920 he acquired a three-wheeler car. There were few cars and few telephones. Communication centred around the Silverton telephone exchange, run by a well-meaning lady who knew only too well who the doctor had been called to see and probably how the patient was

getting on! The doctor recalled calling home and being told that his wife was out, but 'could he pick up some sausages from the butcher on his way home?' – an example of the first message answering service in the village? One day a week a trip round the valley took in Upton Pyne. If the doctor was needed at a house, there would be something red hanging on the hedge – a curious initiative which was used to attract attention and which involved anything from tablecloths to red petticoats. The occasional mistake was made when an item of clothing from the washing line landed unintentionally on the hedge, resulting in the arrival of the doctor at the front door.

Visits were more numerous in those days. The opportunity to observe patients in their own homes often provided important clues as to the cause of the problem. The volume of patient contacts and pressure on time in modern practice makes this activity a rare event, a loss perhaps for doctors and patients.

Hederman was a great lover of country pursuits. He had a mile of fishing rights on the Exe and was devastated by the blight that took out the salmon around 1970. He firmly believed that the cause was pollution. He continued to shoot regularly well into retirement and complained in his eighties that if he raised his 12-bore, looked into the sun, with his gundog straining and tied to his waist he could feel a bit giddy! His style fitted the times admirably. If people told him they thought they had a 'touch of the flu' he would suggest that he was the doctor and that he would decide what was wrong with them! His cough medicine was highly effective and black in colour. The reason it stopped the cough was the inclusion of a 6th of a grain of heroin. Its powerful antitussive action was a well-known side effect, the product was a proper commercial medicine. The patients had no idea of it's content and if they started to show a liking for it, then the addition of tincture of aesfetida made their breath smell so awful that their spouses complained and they stopped taking it. There was no problem with drug abuse in those days. There was little going on in the village that the doctor was unaware of. Fees would be waived in cases of hardship and support of the sick was encouraged by the able bodied. The doctor's firm but kindly presence was a tonic for many.

In the early days 'panel patients' would attend surgery and queue outside the appropriate door still present today, where a tiny waiting room could house half a dozen waiting patients. Surgeries were open ended and all patients seen. One of the doctors was always on duty and a Saturday evening surgery was usual. Extras stood outside the tiny dispensary which was 'manned' by Lily, the doctor's wife. At times it seemed she would have the correct medicine wrapped in parchment, labelled and sealed with sealing wax before the doctor's prescription was presented! The thin walls and her own knowledge of the patients themselves no doubt gave her a shrewd judgement of what was ordered. Their daughter Mary can remember having to rush to catch a bus in the Square, where she would hand a number of these packages of medicines to the driver, to be delivered to collection points around the outlying villages. The number of medicaments was in marked contrast to the modern formula. Virtually everything was made up as a liquid from a stock bottle and often the effect relied on the strength of personality of the prescriber more than its proven therapeutic value. There were three kinds of aspirin; yellow, blue and red – the content differing only in the colour and only the severely ill qualifying for the red variety!

The caution in these tales of a colourful village character must lie in the understanding that they were given to the author of this article by the doctor himself. The lover of a good story, many recall how the good doctor could spin a good yarn, often against himself. When the time came for him to retire, he went on a long cruise and returned as busy as ever, but never to practice medicine again. Both he and his wife had immensely enjoyed their professional career together but sensed the changes to come. He also felt it would be more difficult for his successor to take over if he was still involved. He had his rural interest and a large workshop to keep him busy. With his retirement came the end of an era in village life. It is therefore fitting that a new close in the village should be named after him.

Dr Hederman's retirement came at a very low point in general practice. Eventually the Doctor's Charter in the late 1960s laid the foundations for the modern and much larger primary-health-care team, working from purpose-built premises. Devon was at the forefront of health centre development and Silverton was to have its own centre in 1972. Partnership changes and an ever-expanding team made the original building more and more cramped. The Health Authority were reluctant to extend or even repair the '60s architecture.

In the end, Wyndham House was built in the car park by one practice and rented under the 'cost rent' scheme to the NHS. The other practice remained in part of the old premises, which were transformed around them to form the new hall in time for the millennium.

The 1990s saw a continuous period of change for general practice. First came 'fundholding' with Wyndham House a pilot practice in a consortium of three rural practices planned to be one of the first. Ideological inequity led to withdrawal from this scheme to join a new Mid Devon group of practices who were not interested in fundholding. This group became very active, eventually taking a wider range of practices into its membership and forming the new Primary Care Group of Mid Devon.

Wyndham House has been actively involved in this development from the beginning, conscious of the need to ensure access to the best resources available for patients in the locality. Technological advance has accompanied all these changes and we look into the next millennium with the hope that the computer links with the hospital and other GPs will lead to increased efficiency, direct communication and ever higher standards. Computer-aided diagnosis and management will help the team offer up-to-date care. As a response to increasing demand, we have also seen the introduction of an out-of-hours service. The Silverton doctors all take their turn doing 'shifts'. NHS Direct has been launched but its place in local health care is not yet clear. The challenge for all involved is to try to maintain a personal service.

Top: *Wyndam House Surgery.*
Above: *A modern view of Silverton House, the former Silverton surgery.* (Both J. Tree)

Chapter 11
Memories from America

The following chapter has been edited from an audio tape sent from their home in Kings City, Oregon, USA by Bill Barker and his wife Audrey (née Poole):

I lived in Exeter Road in the 1920s. Our house was number four, later becoming number eight when the numbers were changed. Across the street from our house was a playground where the boys from school would play soccer and other games. This area now, as it has done for many years, contains four houses. Exeter Road was fully thatched at that time, and as a child I remember Mr and Mrs Sanders of The Three Tuns giving a party each Christmas for the village children. We always looked forward to this because in those depression days, there really wasn't much entertainment for any of us.

A victory celebration in King Street after the Second World War.

Across the street and to the left Mr and Mrs Davey and family lived. They occupied one part of the house, and the other part was a stable for their horses. The Daveys had no mechanised delivery vehicles at that time, just horses and carts. Next to the Daveys was the Frankpitts' slaughterhouse. Every Tuesday and Friday the Frankpitts slaughtered the animals for meat, which they sold in their butcher's shop. I can remember hearing the animals screeching, or it sounded like that to me, then there would be a shot, and then quiet. This was during the years before the war, but during the war this stopped because of food rationing.

Across the street from the slaughterhouse was the Faraday House, which burned in the thirties when I was quite young. I can remember the house just burning, and the old pump engine, with all the men of the village pumping the water, but of course it was disastrous and the house was burned to the ground.

Further on down the street was the boys' school on the right, which had a rather small enclosed playground. I remember going there to have an inoculation for diphtheria because at that time there was quite a scare in the village and all children had to be inoculated. On the left of Exeter Road lived Mr Seward, the farmer.

Perratt's Shop was where everyone bought their groceries at that time, and a great variety of items could be purchased here. Wartime rationing made a lot of difference to what we could buy, and people shopped wherever they could find something.

In the Square was Frankpitt's butchers shop and Stradling's bakery, part of which eventually became a Post Office. On Good Friday the Stradling bakery always stayed open until noon so that everyone could get hot-cross buns. This was quite a tradition in those days and I think most people adhered to it. The Post Office remained part of the baker's shop until Miss Bertha Stradling became Postmistress when it moved to the left in Fore Street. I can first remember the Post Office on the opposite corner from the war memorial, and it was there for many years.

The church bells rang every Sunday. They woke us up in time for everyone to get to Communion at eight o'clock, and they pealed again at eleven o'clock for that church service. In those days they would have a service at half-past two in the afternoon for the children, which most children attended.

During the summer when the farmers cut the wheat, oats and the barley in the fields, the boys enjoyed running after the rabbits. When the cutters went through and cut the grain, the rabbits would of course escape and everybody would run and try to catch them. It was really quite

View of Symonds Farm and Perratt's shop and a reciept from the latter, dated 1881.

The centre of the village in the 1930s, with Perratt's shop on the left, and the first cottage in Fore Street, at that time the two Bending sisters' shop and Post Office.

The corner of School Road and Fore Street in the 1920s.

Frankpitt's butchers shop.

The Three Tuns Inn in Exeter Road before the Faraday House in the background was burnt down in the 1930s.

A gathering in the Square possibly after 1920 as the war memorial can be seen.

An empty square in the 1920s, with the fire station on the left by the church path, and Stradling's bakery on the right.

The Square, a modern view, 2000. (J. Tree)

Davey's hauliers tarring the road for the council. Mr William Davey with the horse, his eldest son Reg behind and his second son Fred with the lorry.

The Davey house in Exeter Road with Olive Davey in the doorway and her mother Mrs Polly Davey on the steps. The family were hauliers using horses and carts at this time.

surprising how many were caught, but not often did a person get one and take it home. During the war these rabbits were highly sought after, because it supplemented our very plain diet.

Another tradition was 11 November, and the Sunday closest to that date when there was a service at the war memorial in the Square. All the Boy Scouts, Girl Guides, Brownies, Cub Scouts, etc., gathered there along with all the veterans and the Village Band, for a service. Then all the participants would walk to the church for a full service.

In one of the cottages across from the memorial lived Archie Tremlett. Archie was the local blacksmith and he shod all the horses in the area, and was also the ironmonger. I remember going past his forge in Tiverton Road, across from the Finch house (now 'Wayside'), and seeing the bellows and the fire and how hot it all was. Seeing him work with iron was at the time quite ordinary, but in this day and age it would be a most interesting place to be. Notices of various events were announced by the town crier. I don't remember the name of this man, but he would walk around the village, and stand and ring his bell, and say 'Oyez, oyez' and he would make his announcement.

Before the Second World War peddlers came from Brittany, and they would come loaded with onions and garlic and other fruits and vegetables, which they would sell in Devon villages. Many people went to the farm to get their milk, butter, eggs and their cream, but old Mr Passmore also delivered milk from his farm, which was on the way towards the mill.

I remember the Sunday School outings we had in the summertime, getting the charabancs to Teignmouth or Dawlish, which was considered to be a lot of fun. The Christmas parties at the New Hall, with a very tall Christmas Tree – or at least it seemed so to me. [I also remember] the jumble sales, the fêtes and the carnivals that we had in the wintertime with the dray horses being decorated by the owners; the Jubilee of Queen Mary and King George V, the bonfire on Criss Cross, all the bonfires which we saw had been lit on very high peaks all around Devonshire. I remember walking to Criss Cross at night with my parents and seeing the bonfires which were quite a sight. I still have the mug that most children received, in memory of that day.

In about 1940 we had our first troops in Silverton. They were British troops, and they were billeted in the field just on the other side of Cockhayne House. When Exeter was bombed it could be heard from Silverton, and we spent many a night under the stairs. I will never forget seeing Exeter burning, which seemed to be from one end to another. Rationing was having an affect on all

Top: Fire at Mr Faraday's cottage as shown in a newspaper at the time.

Above: Archie Tremlett's forge, from a painting by Anthony Swain.

Left: Gravestone of Archie Tremlett and his nephew Harry.

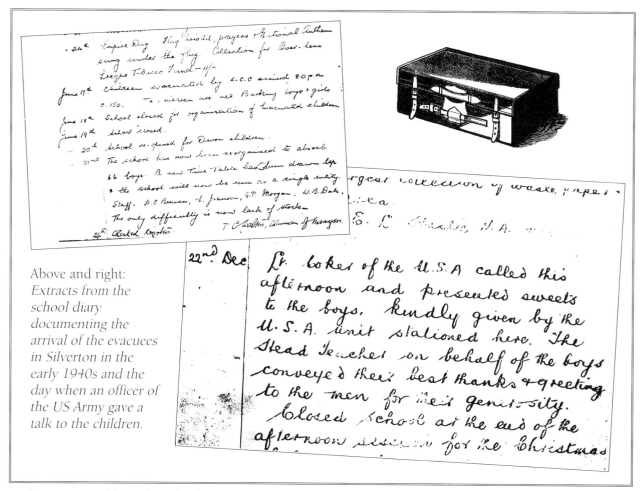

Above and right:
*Extracts from the
school diary
documenting the
arrival of the evacuees
in Silverton in the
early 1940s and the
day when an officer of
the US Army gave a
talk to the children.*

of us. We could not buy the food we had in the past, and our clothes were rationed so we all learned to darn and make do; there was very little petrol, so most of us rode our bikes. Many people put their cars up on blocks and there they stayed until the end of the war.

Many of the villagers worked in the Torpedo factory at Stoke Canon. My mother was conscripted to work there, and I remember her being told that she had worked on the torpedo which had sunk the Graf Spee.

The Americans came in November of 1943 and their lorries stopped all along Exeter Road, almost filling the whole village. They were billeted in the same field next to Cockhayne that had been used previously by the British troops. The 953rd Field Artillery Battalion had arrived in England after three days waiting for the fog to lift enough for their ship to berth at Liverpool harbour. From here the men were transported by train to Silverton Station, and by lorry to the village. Bill recalls that his truck stopped by 8 Exeter Road and a lady came out and had a pitcher full of hot tea and some mugs with which she served our truck. This was Mrs Eva Poole, his future mother-in-law.

The firing batteries, Battery 'A', Battery 'B' and Battery 'C' were billeted in Silverton, whilst the Headquarters, and the Service Battery went to Thorverton.

On the first Sunday that we were in Thorverton, about 25 of us marched down to the village church and one of the sextants saw us coming and led us down to the front. We were a mixture of Roman Catholics and Protestants but the rector looked down and saw all these Yanks sitting there and he said, 'Welcome to Thorverton. 'I had planned a different sermon but as you are here I am going to forget it and give you a history of the Village and the Church building'.

I was transferred to 'B' Battery, and so to Silverton and on the Saturday night a couple of us went to the village dance in the New Hall, where I met my future wife. The village people had no idea what to expect from us, and of course we had very little idea what to expect from them. However, they soon began to see that we weren't all Chicago gangsters and we were just young men far from home, as were their brothers and sons, cousins etc., and we began to form a lot of very fine friendships.

I was intrigued by the surrounding country; it was absolutely beautiful. Although the 953rd was a Brookland National Guard Unit, I was from the state of Kansas which is further from New York than London is. Kansas was a prairie state, and all

Charabanc outing, 1920s, and (inset) some Silverton gentlemen on an outing in a Devon General bus, 1920s.

these beautiful rolling hills, very narrow lanes and hedgerows and thatched roofs, with which you are so familiar, were absolutely new to me. I remember that we finally got used to the warm beer and thoroughly enjoyed our stay.

We were very impressed with how the English were absolutely certain of victory – there was no doubt in their minds as to who would win the war and everything was scheduled and put into the war effort.

I went into Exeter with Audrey my future wife many times. She worked in a grocery office and I would meet her and go to dinner, the cinema or to Exeter College where there was a US Naval dance band. The dances lasted until after the last bus left Exeter for Silverton, so I engaged Mr Ayshford to come and collect us.

It was in the City of Exeter that we all saw our first bomb damage. This really sobered us very quickly and we began to realise really what was ahead of us. We eventually had to pack everything up and get ready to leave. Everybody was confined to the barracks either at Thorverton or Silverton, until five days before D-Day when we were taken down to the beaches and put on ships, etc. I was very fortunate and survived the invasion. I got into the Battle of the Bulge and I spent over two weeks in the same fox-hole. When they

finally got me out and back to the outfit, I rested up and was given leave of absence. I managed to get back to England, which was just like coming home, but then I had to return to combat, and ended up in Czechoslovakia. I was eventually given permission to return to England, and to get married to Audrey on a Saturday, but I had to leave her on the Tuesday to go to the Pacific for training. Luckily the war ended and a few months later Audrey joined me in Kansas.

We have returned to England several times, and our two daughters have accompanied us. They were warmly welcomed and had an absolutely fabulous time playing with the English children. When the rector of the church saw our daughters in Sunday School, he asked my oldest daughter to read the Scripture, saying that the children might as well hear the Scriptures read with an American accent!

Men from Silverton working on the construction of houses, believed to be the first council houses to be built in Silverton, at Lily Lake, c.1928.

Fore Street in 1910. The large house on the left was called Holmans, and was owned by the Savery family who were woollen drapers and cloth dealers.

Chapter 12
Notes and Articles

Two well-known Silvertonians Ted Ayshford (1897-1988) and Ron Bowerman (1916-) have written an account of past times. Here is a selection.

Little School (1920) Three was the age to go to school. My Aunt was an assistant teacher and Mrs Thomas was in charge. The 3Rs were instilled with tolerance, tables and alphabet by rote. I still mentally recite the ABC backwards to check a letter sequence. Learning was interspersed by periods of relaxation, heads on desk, eyes closed, peace reigned! Respect for the countryside was absorbed rather than taught, as was a code of conduct, reinforced by family upbringing. (RB)

Boys' School By the time we reached the age of six or seven we were able to read, write and spell. Mr Fallon the headmaster was very strict, as was his wife, the headmistress at the Girls' School, but they were both splendid at their jobs. He did not hesitate to give two on each hand with the cane, but that was all the better for us. There were football and cricket teams and we played Bradnich and Thorverton. Every so often Mr Fallon took me out to Pitt Farm on the Rifle Range for an hour. The school leaving age was 13. (TA)

The higher playground for the school was behind the war memorial but the surface was not good for many games. The 'Rec.' opposite Church Row (before the bungalows were built) was the favourite venue for all games - football in the winter with coats for goalposts, and cricket in the summertime when a huge boulder was the stumps. All ages in the teams - kids, teenagers and adults - everyone mucked in. There was some 'agro' caused by the ball going over the fencing into an orchard owned by two spinsters. If you went to retrieve it, you would be chased by an irate woman with a broom (an earlier Norah Batty!).

Hoops were another favourite; wooden ones, or if one was lucky enough to earn a shilling, Archie Tremlett the local blacksmith would fashion an iron hoop complete with a metal rod while one stood and watched in awe. (RB)

Roads and Pavements The roads were all dirt and all traffic drove in the middle so of course there were two ruts and the grass would grow in the centre and [along the] sides. Every so often council men would come along with their diggers and level them over. The streets were covered with a layer of stones, well watered and a big steamroller would roll them down. The only vehicles were carts, wagons and farm implements drawn by horses. (TA)

The pavements were originally cobble as were most of the yards and driveways - the bed of the Exe being the most likely source of material. I can recall seeing carts loaded with cobbles, dripping water. (RB)

Above: *Mr William Davey of Mudford House, 9 Exeter Road, c.1912, with the old mail cart he used to drive to Exeter after a day's work. He would leave Silverton in the evening at approximately 7p.m. to get to Exeter to collect the mail, putting up at Parker's Garage which was situated in St Sidwell. After collecting the mail in the early hours of the morning, he would make his first delivery at Cowley, then on to Upton Pyne, Brampford Speke, Thorverton and finally arriving at Silverton about 6a.m. before carrying on with his day's work as haulage contractor. William Davey was the founder of what was later known Wm. Davey and Sons.*

A group of lads outside Ayshford's Garage c.1930.
Left to right: Bill Saunders, Jack Haydon, Percy Saunders, Percy Carpenter, Bert Wood,
Ralph Andrews.

George Stradling and Ralph Andrews in George's MG sports car. Included in the photograph are Bill
and Percy Saunders, Ron Bowerman and Wilf Ball on the motorcycle.

The Three Tuns in Exeter Road in the 1930s.

Pubs   There were three public houses and one cider house. You could have a pint at 6.00a.m. or 11 or12 at night if they were still up. The Three Tuns was at one time a coaching stop for changing horses [on the way] from Plymouth to London. The only way from Silverton was up over Criss Cross. I recall that up the hill big stones stuck out of the road. My brother and his friends from Bristol always came off their motorcycles trying to climb the hill. (TA)

Garage   Mr Ted Ayshford's garage was the first to appear in the village. The two petrol pumps were hand operated - Pratt's Ethyl and Shell Mex at 1s.3d. a gallon (about 7 pence). The delivery pipe had to be lifted up a couple of times to ensure all the fuel was emptied. He hired cars out and bought in motor vehicles, particularly motorbikes. (RB)

The Bowerman Family   I lived next but one to the garage with my parents and two sisters. My father was a postman and although disabled in the Great War still played the violin, piano, cornet and most other musical instruments. He ran the Temperance Band and taught anyone willing to try their skill - the attempt to teach me the piano was a complete failure, and I must have been a great disappointment. (RB)

The Dymond Family   Mr Charles Dymond, one of four bakers in the village, was a friend of my father's and they endeavoured to improve the quality of life by organisations like the Band of Hope and the Rechabites - the demon drink being the main enemy. People were persuaded to sign the pledge, with what success rate I have no idea, but they tried.

Mr Dymond's offspring were clever. Percy, the elder boy, went into journalism and became Editor of one of the leading Irish daily newspapers. G.E. (or Ted) [was] my age, [and] when quite young informed my mother he did not play with naughty boys! How I had incurred his displeasure is not known. Ted was academically inclined and did well at school. He took his 'Matric' and was teaching until war in 1939 changed our careers. He was a member of the Territorial Army, as were several Silverton lads. They were involved early, experiencing Dunkirk, Narvik, the Far East and Burma. Ted ended the war a Major and then went into the Diplomatic Service. (RB)

Right: *Fred Glanville was owner of Central Garage in School Road until his death in 1953.*

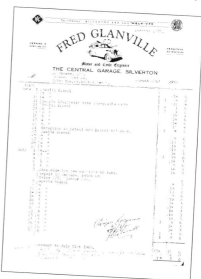

The Temperance Band taken in the orchard, owned by the Bowerman Family, behind the site of the New Hall. Ralph Bowerman is on the far right with baton and founded the band in 1900. It continued until 1910.

Above: *A tea party at the Rectory in Coach Road for the Temperance Society, with the band seated at the table.*
Right: *One of the original pledges that all members of the Temperance Society would have signed before joining.*

Boot and Shoe Makers   Next to the Audit Room was my grandfather's shop. He came to Silverton around 1880, having learnt his trade in Birmingham.

The returns from the boot and shoe business were slow, farmers [being] particularly loathe to pay bills. He embarked on extra lines, hiring out bicycles, penny-farthings, then the more sophisticated types, even racing machines, with boxwood rims for lightness. Paraffin was in constant demand, as oil lamps were the main means of illumination, and carbide for acetylene gas cycle lamps. On entering the shop door two bells would ring, one on the door, and another in the living quarters, activated by wires and pulleys. The walls were wood-panelled and varnished, a long solid wood counter extended the length of the shop, its width about 30 inches; along the inside were inserted rulers, to enable lengths of cloth to be measured. Grandmother sold drapery, etc. On the wall behind, glazed cupboards with the same rich-coloured wood contained ribbons, cottons and, I believe, stiffening materials for hats. Along one wall stood chairs and foot stools for trying on boots and shoes, a selection of shoe horns and buttonhooks (ladies' boots were often fastened by buttons). At the far end another door led to a stone-paved room, where cycles were repaired, and wooden planking covered what I understood to be a disused well.

Narrow wooden stairs at the rear of the shop gave access to the workroom; here sat men engrossed in the craft of making and repairing boots and shoes. They sat around a low table, under which was a metal container of dark liquid (water in fact). As a youngster looking in on this sight it seemed like a scene from Snow White. The men had sprigs held in their mouths which they extracted as required to hammer into the leather. Now and again a piece of leather would be plucked from the liquid after softening. The only sound was the smack of hammer on leather (difficult to gossip with a mouth full of nails). The room next door contained the machine for stitching, another for making button holes, one for sharpening knives [and] others whose function I never discovered.

My grandfather was tolerant of me, although very strict [and] almost tyrannical towards my father and aunt. They were both talented in music and art which my grandfather considered to be the 'pastime of parasites'. He did have a gramophone, 'His Master's Voice' type, with wax cylinders, on which he played songs by Melba and Peter Dawson. The Laughing Policeman was my early favourite. (RB)

Mr C. Frost's Coalyard, Bakery and Cider Press   The coalyard and bakery of Mr C. Frost was an unlikely combination. Joining the back of the building was a cider press, and a device for cutting up apples. A layer of straw was laid on a wooden platform [and] on this was shovelled a layer of apples, then more straw and more apples, until what was called a cheese took shape, maybe four foot high. A heavy wooden construction was lowered over a large wooden worm, which came up through the centre of the cheese. The sides were sheared off with a huge knife as used for cutting hay. The debris was cleared away, then a pony harnessed to a pole attached to the top of the press. The poor beast was blinkered and led around in a circle, causing the cheese to be compressed. The apple juice ran out to be collected in a gutter which surrounded the base and then [ran] via a funnel into barrels.

Coming home from school one day Jock and I were watching this process. He decided he would have a taste, so lying down beneath the funnel guided the liquid into his mouth, his verdict – delicious – so he had another go. No doubt I would have joined him but for the brain washing about strong drink. A little later he decided he had better go home (his mother kept a shop in High Street). Before he could make it, however, and sprint as he may, the juice was the winner! We all wore short trousers then, and his embarrassment was all too visible.

My mother often made saffron cake. This required yeast, and as a lover of the cake I needed no urging to fetch the necessary from Mr Frost. It was often three penny-worth, and he would put the coins on one side of the scales, and yeast on the other until they balanced – simple but effective!

The floor of Mr Frost's bakery was cobbled. One entered down two steps and into a long room with a heavy wooden table, and [there was] an oven at the far end. I think bread was the only thing made. Old Mr Frost seemed large from a kid's perspective. His waist was enveloped by an off-white flour bag. I do not remember seeing him outside the bakery. (RB)

The Carrier   We had a carrier who went to Exeter every Friday and brought back goods for the village. He had a horse and covered wagon and his name was Batte Thomas. He would put up at a pub in Paul Street, Exeter. When he left in the evening he was sometimes a bit 'sozzled', but he would get up and call his horse and they left for home. That horse knew his job for he would stop at every public house on the way. I remember once his people having to go down Up Exe Hill to pick up things that had rolled off the wagon. (TA)

A view taken outside the Audit Rooms with Mr Bowerman's boot repair shop on the right. Note the ornate oil street lamp.

An early view of Fore Street with a group standing outside the Post Office, in it's earliest known location. It is interesting to note the very irregular pavements.

Mr Charles Frost's bakery and cider pound. This gentleman also had a coal yard at the rear of the premises. The pound has since been converted into a dwelling.

Baker's Cottage in 1999.

Silverton Carnival This will take some time to tell, as it was such a great night - tableaux-decorated cycles and walking costumes and any amount of side-shows. The people used to get lorries or any vehicles decorated. My father would put on his blacksmith's shop - complete with fire and anvil and his apprentice with sledgehammer and oh boy did they send the sparks flying! Mr mother's tableaux was dress-making and millinery with all her apprentices - she had about eight. Collecting boxes were all over the place. The proceeds went to the hospital. The Manager at Silverton Paper Mill would send up to say that the villagers could have what paper they wanted. Rolls of coloured paper 2" and 3" wide were used to make into rosettes and paper chains, and everything looked lovely. All the tableaux, decorated cycles and walking costumes would parade at the Girls' School for judging. After that was over, the torchlit procession would start off and a Mr Walland would head the procession on horseback with a pet fox on his shoulder, or on the saddle. Then would come the Town Band, Fire Engine and so on. The procession would go up Fore Street and High Bullen (now High Street) and would turn around at the big pond and go down Back Lane (now King Street) and up Tiverton Road to the Square. They were never short of torches so everywhere was a blaze of light. I should have mentioned that the Temperance Band played halfway back in the procession. After it was over,

people would go to the Audit Room for the final dance until 12 midnight - no one was allowed to go over that on a Saturday night. (TA)

Top: *The crowning of a Silverton Carnival Queen, Miss Helen Piney, by Mrs Hedderman, in the New Hall, 1957.*
Left to right: Mr G. French, Mrs Frost, Mrs Webb, Mrs Brookes, Mrs Vittles, Mrs Hutchings, Mrs Pike,
Mr W. Furbear, Mrs Sutton, ?; with Mrs Edwards seated. The children are, left to right: Margaret Western,
Peter Davies and Glynis Tree.
Centre: *A Silverton Carnival float, c.1947. Left to right: Man in bed - Mr Brady, his wife Elsie, Mrs Lovell,*
Mrs F. Vittles, Mr F. Sutton and his mother Mary plus children.
Above: *A group of children dressed for the village carnival, complete with dog, c.1910.*
Left to right, girls at back: A. Sanders, ?, Mollie Dart, Evelyn Priddle;
boys at front: Percy Frankpitt, Donald Jennings, Stanly Perratt, Albert Sanders, Ted Frankpitt.

Clockwise from top left: *The first view of Silverton seen by travellers from the Tiverton direction. A hay rick has been built in the field beside Pembridge Cottage; A view of Pitt Farm in Tiverton Road taken from the 1915 Silverton Estate sale catalogue; Hedge trimming on the main Exeter to Tiverton road, at Burn Farm, in 1952. Looking towards Bickleigh, the smoke from a steam train can be seen in the valley. Cyril Knowles is driving the Ferguson tractor, Harry Broom is positioning the cutter, and Mr Pyle, the farmer, is counter-balancing the machine. (courtesy* Mid Devon Gazette*); Mr Woolway senior stitching sheeves of corn on Ash Farm; A 'carter' thought to be Bill Nicholls at Land Farm in the 1920s.*

Farms Before the First World War most farmers had two horsemen, one shepherd and one yardman to look after the cows, etc. Cows going to market were driven and two drovers would take over at Stoke Woods. The horses were kept for ploughing and other work on the farm. The men had their houses rent free, and anything that was grown on the farm. In those days the corn was cut with a binder. It threw out the sheaves and there was always help to stitch them up. They were often unlucky and if the weather was wet the corn turned black. Farmers could only get a threshing machine once a year. Towards the end of the war things began to change, and tractors could be seen on the farms. (TA)

Horse hoeing the steep field opposite Burn Farm in 1962.
Harry Broom is at the rear, and Bill Wannel leading 'Lion' the horse. (Bernard and Gwen Hawkins)

Haymaking at White Cow Field, Burn Farm, 1950. Mr Pyle is standing on the hay rick.
(courtesy *Mid Devon Gazette*)

Football There was so much talent in the village; three soccer teams, as well as supplying Tiverton Town with four players. The teams had very good support, especially for cup matches, and were successful, often against opposition in higher leagues. We played Tiverton Town in one final and won the cup, much to the chagrin of the village lads who played for Tivvy.

Herbert 'Nimmy' Pearce was a player with tremendous skill, an inside forward in those days. Jimmy Dymond was centre half and dominated the mid field. Later I had moved to right back and played beside 'Dutchie' (Francis Kenshole). The player in front of me was Tiny Williams at right half. His energy was boundless and he would come to a match after ploughing all morning, walking behind two mighty horses. His legs were bow shaped, and he used them like a scythe, to collect any player and ball who tried to pass him. Bill 'Bussie' Carpenter was the youngest of a family of goalkeepers – fathers and uncles all played in that position. He was not very tall but very little passed him. [He had] one failing – he would get bored if there was not much for him to do; when the ball came his way he would deliberately throw it to the opposition to get a shot back.

We had two brilliant wingers. One of these, Walter 'Tiggy' Selley who played on the left, could shoot from a couple of yards inside the corner flag, the ball not rising more than a couple of feet until it hit the back of the net – this was with a heavy leather ball.

The team had a blend of youth and experience, with players in their thirties and some about half that age. [There were] Perce Saunders (Nobby) and Len, and his younger brother Bill Rookes, who was in the RAF at Boscombe Down but who travelled home at weekends on his motorbike to play. Ralph Hutchings, a senior player, kept a supervisory eye on behaviour at away matches. George, and later Jack Rosser, were skillful members. It was a fight to maintain a place as there were always people available to cover any loss of form. The pitch was on a field rented from a farmer at Hayne, about a mile and a half from the Berry. It was level and full size. When wet, the leather ball absorbed a lot of moisture, increasing its weight. Strong neck muscles and the right technique were required when heading a ball. I remember on one occasion when Jimmy Dymond took a penalty with a heavy ball. The keeper saved the shot, but could not prevent himself from being lifted to the back of the net.

Transport for away matches was provided by Mr Ted Ayshford in two American cars, a Chrysler which seated seven and an Essex which could take six. The Chrysler was a powerful car. A motorbike passed, and there was a discussion as to its manufacture, Ted put his foot down and we caught up with the rider in a very short time, much to his surprise. There were no substitutes in our day, so the two cars were adequate.

I was sent off only once; that was a cup match at Clyst Hydon and a team we had not played before. Shortly into the match, a red-headed player came charging at me. I took the ball off him without much difficulty, cleared up field then found myself being attacked from behind. The blows were more wild than hurtful. I managed one in reply which sat him on the grass. The referee sent us both off. I was too surprised to even protest. Subsequently, at the inquiry where Ralph Hutchings presented my case, it was found the red-headed gent trained on cider, and was unstable. He was suspended and I was exonerated.

We did not play Broadclyst or Thorverton much unless in Cup competitions. We were well aware of the reputations of their players. Tom Bond, Tom Moore and Fido Pearce from Broadclyst (Indian Country), Davis Brothers and Ron Edworthy at Thorverton. At Willand there were three Trevlian brothers. Their mother used to run the touchline with an umbrella, with which to clobber anyone who hurt the youngest of the trio, who played on the wing. (RB)

Top: *Silverton United football team 1933-34. Left to right, back row: Bill Carpenter (senr), Percy Williams, Francis Kenshole, Herbert Pearce, William Tweedie, Victor Strong, Edwin Gooding, Bert Wood, Percy Hine, Bill Nicholls, George Kenshole; front: Bill Rookes, Ralph Hutchings, Harry Bulley, Bill Carpenter (junr), Jack Tree.*
Above: *Silverton Football Team 1949-50 and their officials.*

A view of Fore Street showing an oil street lamp as would have been attended to by the lamp-lighter.

GLOBAL WARMING IN 1911!

Mr Francis George Heath writes from 'The Grange', Silverton, on 8 January 1911:

Probably the most extraordinary evidence of the unique character of this winter produced by it's abnormal mildness and moistness is found in the fact that today I have in my orchard hedge here a number of hollies bursting into leaf bud, and several with new leaf growth nearly an inch long! This fact is especially remarkable because of all our evergreens the holly is usually the latest to re-bud, seldom doing so, even in early springs, before April or May. In the same orchard I have had scores of primroses for many weeks past in full blossom. Weeds - as other wild flowers are contemptuously called - are growing apace, and even a bordering row of the beautiful golden cyprus (Cupressus macrocarplutea) is steadily advancing oblivious of the circumstances that the calendar labels the time, January the eighth!

DUTIES OF THE LAMP LIGHTER IN THE 1920s
TAKEN FROM PARISH COUNCIL MINUTES

All cases to be cleaned inside before putting into containers and chimneys. Cases and chimneys and lamps to be kept clean during the lighting season and to leave all lamp cases and chimneys and lamps clean at the end of the season of lighting, and store chimneys and lamps in the engine house.

All lamps to be lighted at dusk each night and to be kept lighted until ten o'clock each night. To stop lighting five nights before the full moon, but must be lighted first night after the full moon and at any other time if required by the committee. Time of payment will begin at the first night of lighting and to stop at the last night of lighting, of which the committee will decide.

SILVERTON SCAVENGING
TAKEN FROM PARISH COUNCIL MINUTES

Cleaning Streets, Footpaths, Gutters etc. in the first quarter of the 20th century.

Man to commence work at 7a.m., leave work at 5p.m. each Saturday. All streets and footpaths to be swept from the end cottage in High Street to the end of buildings opposite Glebe Cottage. Through Balls Lane, from Mrs. Spalding's gate to Mr. Paul's door in Upexe Road to the large doors of Miss. Rowells in Welsh Road on the boys' playground side to Mr. Perratt's corner to the end cottage in Tiverton Road, including Parsonage Lane and King Street. The sides of the roads and streets to be properly cleaned.

All gullies under all water taps in the village to be cleaned out every Saturday including the small pits in the gutter in High Bullen by the water tap, by Mrs. B. Selley's pit, by pipe across road by the Lamb.

The gutter from the pond in High Street through the town to Mr. Gale's large doors in Tiverton Road including all inlets and outlets to be cleaned every Saturday, the gutter should be swept clean. The pools must be cleaned out under each tap as often as necessary and on no account should mud be allowed to accumulate much at a time in case of using the pits in case of fire. When cleaning out the mud to be put in the cart and not in the road. Man to find all tools in connection with the work. Man to help load after finishing sweeping. Start at 2 p.m., man with horse and cart to commence collecting all the horse manure in the village and the sweepings including calling at the two houses in Welsh Road and at Mr. Vosper's each Saturday and to cart all of it to Silverton Park. Each Saturday to a suitable place provided by the contractor and approved by the Parochial Council.

The contractor to find all tools in connection with the work.

NOTE FROM BRAMPFORD SPEKE BURIAL REGISTER, 27 MARCH 1848

Thomas Powell of the Parish of Silverton. Age 69. By Coroners warrant. Verdict 'Found Drowned' Deceased was identified by Mr. E.D. Puddicombe of Silverton, Surgeon, as his late servant who had been missing since 27th. January. On that day he had been sent to Nether Exe with his Master's horse and left that place to return home on foot at about 8 o'clock p.m. He enquired his road at a cottage leading to the river as late as 12 p.m. (sic) and was not seen or heard of again until his body was found in the River Exe and landed in the Parish of Brampford Speke on 25th. March.

Subscribers

John Abrahams, Winford, North Somerset
David W. Abrahams, Hele, Exeter, Devon
Lynda S. Ahmad, Southampton, Hampshire
Joyce M. G. Austin, Silverton, Devon
Philip Avery, Silverton, Devon
Daniel and Rachel Ayshford, Silverton, Devon
Thomas E. Ayshford, Perth, Canada
James E. Ayshford, Exeter, Devon
Joan K. Ayshford, Silverton, Devon
Richard E. Ayshford, Montreal, Canada
Francis (Frank) Ayshford, Walton-On-Thames,
    Surrey
Mrs M. M. Babbington, Silverton, Devon
Linda Bailey, Newfoundland, Canada
Michael Baker, Aishe Barton, Silverton, Devon
Reggie Ball, Kingsteignton, Devon
Edward C. Ball, Willand, Devon
Aurelia C. R. Ball (née Wreford)
Gill Bamforth, Silverton, Devon
Susan Banks, Silverton, Devon
Audrey Poole Barker, Oregon, USA
Audrey Barker (née Poole) Betty Scagell (née Poole),
    born Silverton, Devon
Wilf and Joan Barnes, Silverton, Devon
Peter Barons, Silverton, Devon
Davina and Richard Barron, Silverton, Devon
Patricia A. Barron, Silverton, Devon
Drs John and Anne Bate, Silverton, Devon
Mr Jeremy and Mrs Jane Bazley, Middleford,
    Silverton, Devon
Ros and Steve Bennett, Silverton, Devon
Nada Bibey, Silverton, Devon
Victor G. Blatchford
Helen Boucher (née Ayshford), formerly of
    Silverton, Devon
Adam Sadler Bowles, Calgary, formerly from
    Silverton, Devon
Mrs Patricia Mary Bradford, Exeter, Devon/
    descendant of Dymond's
Donald I. and Nancy Brady, Silverton, Devon
Mr and Mrs P. Brailey, Silverton, Devon
Debbie and Nigel Brett, Silverton, Devon
Frances Brewer, Silverton, Devon
Eileen E. Brook, Silverton, Devon
David T. Brook, Four Oaks, West Midlands
Mr E. Brook, Exeter, Devon
Clair M. Broom, Silverton, Devon
Paul and Marilyn Brown, Silverton, Devon
Andrew Bryant, Dover, Kent

Barry Bryant, Ex The Square, Hele, Devon
K. J. Burrow, Bucks Cross, Devon
Gina Bush, Silverton, Devon
Victoria S. Butler, Corsham, Wilts.
Val Butler, Silverton, Devon
Miss Sheila Cameron, Silverton, Devon
Desmond and Barbara Campbell, Silverton, Devon
James T. Carroll
Mr J. A. Catlin, Hamilton, Ontario, Canada
John and Di Channon, Silverton, Devon
Charlotte R. Christie, Silverton, Devon
Isobel R. Christie, Silverton, Devon
Mr William H. Chudley, Formerley of Silverton,
    Devon
Mary Chudley, Silverton, Devon
C. M. Chudley, Silverton, Devon
Chris Chudley, Cullompton, Devon
Stuart J. Chudley, Pinhoe, Exeter, Devon
Roy and Mary Clark, Silverton, Devon
Hazel I. Clarke, Silverton, Devon
Margaret Clough, Silverton, Devon
Richard Cochin and Charlotte Rhodes, Silverton,
    Devon
Philip Cockcram, Exewick, Exeter, Devon
Mr and Mrs T. P. Collings, Silverton, Devon
David A. Conn, Silverton, Devon
Ken and Alice Cooper, Silverton, Devon
Richard B. Cosway, Ellerhayes, Hele, Devon
Dr David Courtenay-Stamp, Silverton, Devon
Peter D. Crabtree, born 10 King Street, Silverton,
    Devon
Dinah Ann Crew, Silverton, Devon
Jacques and Rosemary Croizat, Silverton, Devon
Bill and Sylvia Croome, Silverton, Devon
Dr Malcolm Darch, Rownhams, Hampshire
Minnie Davey, Silverton, Devon
S. E. and S. J. Davidson, Ellerhayes, Hele, Devon
Peter A. Davies, Exminster
Mrs Nora Davies, Fore Street, Silverton, Devon
Mr and Mrs G. Davies, School Road, Silverton,
    Devon
Mr and Mrs E. J. Davies, Silverton, Devon
Peter D. Davies, Silverton, Devon
Mrs J. E. Deguet, Queensland, Australia
Karen Devaraj, Thorverton, Devon
Mrs Edith Diamond, Silverton, Devon
Lyn Dyer, Lympstone, Devon
John Edward Dymond, Northam, W. Australia
Nigel Charles Dymond, Mundaring, W. Australia

Jane Margaret Dymond, W. Australia
Elizabeth Helen Dymond, Perth, W. Australia
Mrs Phyllis E. Dymond, Silverton, Devon
W. G. Edmund, Ouville L'Abbaye, France
Ann Edwards, Stockwell, Silverton, Devon
Maxine Edwards and Richard Money, Silverton, Devon
Joyce E. Eldridge, Silverton, Devon
Richard, Andrea and Steven Ellis, Silverton, Devon
Mr William Ellis, Brampford-Speke, Devon
Mr and Mrs E. John Elston, Silverton, Devon
Jean Farrell, Silverton, Devon
Francis G. Fishleigh, Rewe, Stoke Cannon, Devon
Margaret and Paul Fitzmaurice, Silverton, Devon
Shaun Fitzpatrick, Silverton, Devon
Dominic P. Fleming, Silverton, Devon
Mrs M. J. Follett (née Petherick), Cullompton, Devon
John and Janet Frankpitt, Silverton, Devon
Miss H. M. Fraser, Copplestone, Crediton, Devon
Mr and Mrs F. D. L. Fraser, Greenslinch, Silverton, Devon
Mrs B. A. Freemantle, Silverton, Devon
M. and F. Freemantle, Silverton, Devon
Steven French, Stockleigh English, Devon
Peggy French, Silveton, Devon
Colin French, Lower Washfield, Devon
Terry Furbear
Diane M. Furbear, Gloucestershire
Mr and Mrs M. Gale, Darren and Lisa, Silverton, Devon
Vi Gilham, Silverton, Devon
Michael J. Gill, Thorverton, Devon
Eric Gill, Silverton, Devon
Pearl Gill (née Carpenter), Silverton, Devon
Peter, Jenny and Harriet Gilmour, Silverton, Devon
Christine A. Goodall, Silverton, Devon
Matthew B. Gooding, Silverton, Devon
Bryan and Margaret Gooding, Silverton, Devon
Laurence and Colleen Gooding, Silverton, Devon
Eva E. Gooding, Silverton, Devon
D. G. Gooding and Ms J. M. Baker, Silverton, Devon
The Grange Family, Silverton, Devon
Pauline J. Grant (née Sharland), Reading, Berkshire
Diana Jean Grant-Dalton, Silverton, Devon
Eric Gray, Hayridge Cottage, Silverton, Devon
Jane M. Greed, Silverton, Devon
Colin Green, Silverton, Devon
Mr Colin Green, Silverton, Devon
Mr Malcolm Green, Cullompton, Devon
Caroline W. Greenaway (née Parsons), Tiverton, Devon
Michael and Sheila Griffin, at the Gallery
Peter Gristwood and Celia Bartlett, Orchard Jefferys, Silverton, Devon
Anthea M. Guest, Frieth, Oxon
Ann and Peter Gundry
Hugh Gurney, Barnstaple, Devon
Barbara Hambleton, Silverton, Devon
Andrew J. Hamilton, Silverton, Devon
Stephen A. Hamilton, formerly of Lily Lake/now Oak Close
John and Pam Hardacre, Silverton, Devon

Adrian and Michaela Harris, Ellerhayes, Devon
Naomi Harris, Riseden, Silverton, Devon
Patricia Hawkes, Great Pitt Granary, Silverton, Devon
Alice M. Hawkins, Silverton, Devon
Bernard and Gwen Hawkins, Silverton, Devon
Velmay J. Haydon, Ellerhayes, Hele, Devon
A. R. and M. Haydon, Coach Road, Silverton, Devon
Mark Haydon, Perth, Australia
Gary and Vicki Heap, Garstang, Lancashire
Clare V. Higglesden (née Parsons), Sutton, Surrey
Amanda C. Higman, Cardiff
Jonathan S. Higman, Oxford
Roger K. Higman, Silverton, Devon
Denise E. Hitchings, Silverton, Devon
Derek and Evelyn Holden, Silverton, Devon
Steve and Frances Holden, Tutbury, Staffs
Melissa L. Holder (née Petherick), Cullompton, Devon/formerly of Silverton
Denis and Prissie Holwill, Silverton, Devon
Rae Hoole, Newcourt Road, Silverton, Devon
Brian J. Hooper, Silverton, Devon
Nick and Lorraine Hopkinson, Silverton, Devon
Sally and Lysanne Horrox, London
Nancy Horrox (née Webb), Bucks.
Joan M. Howe, Silverton, Devon
Joy Howell-Jones, Poltimore, Devon
Mrs A. M. Hughes, Silverton, Devon
Susan Hughes (née Vinnicombe)
Monica Hyde (née Dymond), born Silverton, Devon
Shirley M. Hynes, Silverton, Devon
Jane Iffla, Efford House, Shobrooke, Devon
Mrs Elizabeth Islip, Silverton, Devon
Derek and Margaret Jefferson, Silverton, Devon
Anthony and Hannah Jefferson, Tiverton, Devon
O. A. K. Jones, Longdown, Exeter, Devon
Richard H. Jones, Silverton, Devon
John and Eleanor Kiely, Silverton, Devon
Tara Kiely, Silverton, Devon
Lieutenant-Colonel E. G. King, Silverton, Devon
Betty Kirby (née Selley), Queensland, Australia
John H. Knapp, Silverton, Devon
Edie Knight (née Ball), Gloucester
Clare J. Landymore, Wyndham House Surgery, Silverton, Devon
Suzanne Lane, Willand, Devon
David Crispin Langdon, Silverton, Devon
Mrs Phyllis H. Langdon, Thorverton, Devon
Eileen Langford, The Meads, Silverton, Devon
Mr and Mrs Neil Lawson, Silverton, Devon
Brian Le Messurier, Exeter, Devon
Dr Richard Leete, Silverton, Devon
Misses Rhona and Vivien Lewis, Silverton, Devon
Anne Liggins, Silverton, Devon
Cathea D. Lilley (née Wood), Brisbane, Australia
Angela Lingley, Barnstaple, Devon
Mrs C. Lloyd, The Cottage, Greenslinch, Silverton, Devon
Carey Lloyd, Greenslynch, Silverton, Devon
Dave Lloyd, Silverton, Devon
Andrew Luckham, Silverton, Devon
David Lyon-Smith, Silverton, Devon
The Revd Alan MacDonald, Silverton Rectory

SUBSCRIBERS

Katrina A. Macneill

Lindsay and Richard Mallett, Silverton, Devon

Dianne Marshall and Doug Dewdney,
    Victoria, Canada

Katie Maxwell-Hyslop, Silverton, Devon

Robin and Anna Maxwell-Hyslop, Silverton, Devon

Jane Maxwell-Hyslop, Silverton, Devon

Bentley Ann Miller, Silverton, Devon

Elizabeth Milward, Silverton, Devon

Mrs Ann D. Mogridge, Silverton, Devon

Barbara Moody, Silverton, Devon

Peggy Moore, Silverton, Devon

Elfreda E. Morgan, Silverton, Devon

Martin R. Nash, Tintagel, North Cornwall

J. L. Northfield, Silverton, Devon

Mrs Gwen Norton (née coombe), Canterbury, Kent

Jeff and Gill Ody, East Molesey, Surrey

Percy R. Oliver, South Africa

Christine D. Orchard (née Parsons), Muxton,
    Shropshire

David and Christine Packham, Combesatchfield,
    Devon

Mrs Joan Park (née Stradling), Silverton, Devon

Delia Mary Parker, Silverton, Devon

Michael R. H. Parnell, Fulham, London

Claire Parnell, Kingston-Upon-Thames, Surrey

Lorraine Parr, Halberton, Devon

Michael and Pamela Parsons, Silverton, Devon

Andrew M. Parsons, Royal Leamington Spa,
    Warwickshire

R. F. Passmore, Matford, Exeter, Devon

Jennifer Payne, Silverton, Devon

Graham and Rosa Peacock, Orari Gorge, Geraldine,
    New Zealand

Mary R. Pennington, Silverton, Devon

Joan Perratt, Exmouth, Devon

Mr David H. W. Petherick, Silverton, Devon

Jill Phillips, Silverton, Devon

Bill and Joan Piney, Silverton, Devon

John A. M. Plastow, Silverton, Devon

Catherine J. Ponsford (née Parsons), Exminster, Devon

Mrs Kathleen M. Pritchard (née Dymond), Deal, Kent

Paul M. Read, Silverton, Devon

Barbara M. Read, Ashurst, Hampshire

Mrs Mary Read (née Hederman), Radyr, Cardiff

Stephen and Jenny Roach, Silverton, Devon

John T. Rosser, Silverton, Devon

Mr and Mrs James Rundle, Victoria, Australia

Mrs Josephine Saunders, The Garden House,
    Silverton, Devon

R. B. and M. A. Say, Silverton, Devon

Werner and Margarete Schnepp, Exeter, Devon

Myfanwy, Frances and Edmund Scrivener,
    Silverton, Devon

Barbara Selby (née Trump), Bradninch, Devon

Sarah Self, Silverton, Devon

Terry Selley, Silverton, Devon

Grace Selley, Silverton, Devon

Michael Shapcott, Silverton, Devon

Mr Paul Sharman, Killerton, Devon

Marjorie M. Shere, Silverton, Devon

Donald Short, Silverton, Devon

Silverton C. of E. Primary School,

Jean and Clifford Skinner, Silverton, Devon

Laurence A. J. Skinner, Exeter, Devon

Carol A. Skinner, Silverton, Devon

Gladys Slade (née Dymond), Silverton, Devon

Mrs I. R. Smith, Upexe, Thorverton, Devon

Peter and Liz Smith, Silverton, Devon

D. and D. B. Snellgrove, Silverton, Devon

John and Marion Southey, Silverton, Devon

Ian and Heather Sowden, Silverton, Devon

Elaine Stevens, Silverton, Devon

Mary Stickland (née Parsons) and Gillian Parsons

The Stirling Family, Silverton, Devon

June E. Stoneman, Silverton, Devon

Miss J. B. Stradling, Silverton, Devon

Graham N. Street, Silverton, Devon

The Street family, formerly of The Gables, Stockwell,
    Devon

Ron and Sally Sutherland, Silverton, Devon

Phyllis and John Swain, Wayside, Silverton

John Swain, Wayside, Silverton, Devon

Evelyn Y. Symons, Silverton, Devon

Y. and P. Taylor, Norwich, Norfolk

Claire Taylor (née Saunders), formerly of
    Stockwell House, Silverton,

John Teasdale, Newcourt Road, Silverton, Devon

Helen and Michael Thomas, Silverton, Devon

Mrs Rosemarie Thomas (née Petherick), Carmarthen

Shirley A. Thompson, Malton, North Yorkshire

Catherine M. Town, Silverton, Devon

Elizabeth Trebble, Silverton, Devon

Terry, Katie and Cody Tree, Silverton, Devon

Mrs A. Tremlett, Silverton, Devon

Rev Dick Tripp, Governors Bay, New Zealand

David Trump, Stockwell, Silverton, Devon

Roger and Sue Tucker, Silverton, Devon

Phil and Janet Turner, Silverton, Devon

Mary Turner, Tiverton, Devon

Ronald F. Upham, Ilminster, Somerset

Anne and Robert Vanneck, Silverton, Devon

P. R. Vicary, Silverton, Devon

Mr Keith Vinnicombe, Heavitree, Exeter, Devon

Mr Ernest J. and Mrs Alice Vinnicombe (née Ball),
    ex Silverton, Devon

Miss J. Walker, Silverton, Devon

John F. W. Walling, Newton Abbot, Devon

Anthony Watson, former Rector of Silverton

Roger Webb, Shropshire

Frank Webb, Silverton, Devon

Richard and Judith Wheeler, Silverton, Devon

Mr Robert White, Silverton, Devon

Robert C. White, Silverton, Devon

Christopher J. White, Cullompton, Devon

Stuart J. White, Edmonton, London

Mr and Mrs S. J. White, Silverton, Devon

Angela E. White (née Ball), Exeter, Devon

John and Belinda Whitworth, Ford, Silverton

Fiona Winsor, Stockleigh Pomeroy, Devon

Ivan A. Wood, Brisbane, Australia

Stuart Wood, Penarth, South Wales

Gillian Woolacott, South Nutfield, Surrey

G. C. and J. M. Wright, Silverton, Devon

AVAILABLE TO BUY NOW IN THE SERIES

The Book of Addiscombe, In Celebration of a Croydon Parish • Various
The Book of Bampton, A Pictorial History of a Devon Parish • Caroline Seward
The Book of Bickington, From Moor to Shore • Stuart Hands
The Parish Book of Cerne Abbas, Abbey and After • Vivian and Patricia Vale
The Book of Chittlehampton, A North Devon Parish • Various
The Book of Cornwood and Lutton, Photographs and Reminiscences • Compiled by the People of the Parish
The Ellacombe Book, A Portrait of a Torquay Parish • Sydney R. Langmead
The Book of Grampound with Creed • Amy Bane and Mary Oliver
The Book of Hayling Island and Langstone • Various
The Book of High Bickington, A Devon Ridgeway Parish • Avril Stone
The Book of Helston, Ancient Borough and Market Town • Jenkin with Carter
The Book of Ilsington, A Photographic History of the Parish • Dick Wills
Lanner, A Cornish Mining Parish • Scharon Schwartz and Roger Parker
The Book of Lamerton, A Photographic History • Ann Cole and Friends
The Book of Loddiswell, Heart of the South Hams • Various
The Book of Manaton, Portrait of a Dartmoor Parish • Compiled by the People of the Parish
The Book of Meavy, Dartmoor Parish, Village and River • Pauline Hemery
The Book of Minehead with Alcombe • Hilary Binding and Douglas Stevens
The Book of North Newton, In Celebration of a Somerset Parish • Robins & Robins
The Book of Plymtree, The Parish and its People • Tony Eames
The Book of Porlock, A Pictorian Celebration • D. Corner
Postbridge – The Heart of Dartmoor • Reg Bellamy
The Book of Priddy, A Photographic Portrait of Mendip's Highest Village • Various
South Tawton and South Zeal with Sticklepath, 1000 Years Below the Beacon • Roy and Ursula Radford
The Book of Torbay, A Century of Celebration • Frank Pearce
Widecombe-in-the-Moor, A Pictorial History of a Dartmoor Parish • Stephen Woods
Uncle Tom Cobley and All, Widecombe-in-the-Moor • Stephen Woods
Woodbury, The Twentieth Century Revisited • Roger Stokes

SOME OF THE MANY TITLES AVAILABLE 2001

The Book of Bickleigh • Barrie Spencer
The Book of Blandford Forum • Various
The Book of Dawlish • Frank Pearce
The Book of Hemyock • Various
The Book of Hurn • Margaret Phipps
The Lustleigh Book • Tim Hall
The Book of Rattery • Various
The Book of Publow with Pensford • Various
The Book of Severn • Various
The Book of South Stoke • Various
The Book of Sparkwell • Pam James
The Book of Stourton Caundle • Philip Knott
The Book of Watchet • Compiled by David Banks
The Book of West Huntspill • Various

For details of any of the above titles or if you are interested in writing your own community history, please contact: Community Histories Editor, Halsgrove House, Lower Moor Way, Tiverton Business Park, Tiverton, Devon EX16 6SS, England Tel: 01884 243242/e-mail:sales@halsgrove.com
If you are interested in a particular photograph in this volume, it may be possible to supply you with a printout. Please call the above number for information.